# BIOWARFARE
# IN AMERICA

### Jim Keith

Library of Congress Cataloging in Publication Data

Keith, Jim, 1949—
        Biowarfare in America / by Jim Keith.
                    p.      cm.
        ISBN: 1-881532-21-6
        1.      Biological warfare.
        2.      Chemical warfare.
        3.      United States—Defenses.
        4.      World politics—1989-              I.   Title

UG447.8 .H58  1999
358'.38'0973—dc21                                         99-048627

IllumiNet Press
P.O. Box 9002
Atlanta, GA  31106

Printed in the United States of America

# CONTENTS

# INTRODUCTION
## THE THREAT

To begin, let us define our terms. According to a 1969 United Nations report, biological weapons are "living organisms, whatever their nature, or infective material derived from them, which are intended to cause disease or death in man, animals, or plants, and which depend for their effects on their ability to multiply in the person, animal, or plant attacked."

Chemical weapons are, according to the same United Nations report, "chemical substances, whether gaseous, liquid, or solid, which might be employed because of their direct toxic effects on man animals, and plants."

At this time, more than twenty-five countries are developing, or have stockpiles of chemical and biological weapons, in many cases in sufficient quantities to wipe out the entire population of the world. This is no Chicken Little scenario that I am describing, but a fact that must be soberly confronted. These countries are the United States, Libya, North Korea, Iraq, Taiwan, Syria, Israel, Iran, China, Egypt, Vietnam, Laos, Cuba, Bulgaria, India, South Korea, South Africa, Russia, and several countries in the former Soviet bloc. Within the next few years, it is estimated there will be fifty countries with chemical or biological warfare capability, raising the dangers of confrontations using these weapons by a geometric proportion.

While countries are busily engaged in stockpiling deadly chemical and biological agents, we also see an increased incidence of CBW (chemical biological warfare) terrorist attacks by individuals and militant independent groups, including political and religious zealots. There's nothing like a religion of love to turn a man into a murderer, as can be seen by the current wave of terrorism sponsored by the pious.

Although most of these terrorist threats and attacks are not reported widely in the mainstream media, they will be covered in the pages that follow.

We also currently face the deadly threat of what are known in the vernacular as "designer diseases," that is, diseases engineered for warfare purposes that have been either accidentally or intentionally released into the environment.

Although information about the proliferation of man-made diseases is carefully suppressed by governments and the media, there is ample reason to think that some of these diseases are currently loose in the environment, sickening and killing people.

The full import of the CBW threat has not been dealt with by governments, by the media, or by the person in the street. Not only is America unprepared and ignorant of what is happening, but the people in government and scientific professions who do know, who should be warning the American public about the dangers of chemical and biological terrorism, are instead doing their utmost to hide this information from us; information that is vital for our survival. This is information that is known to many scientists and politicians in all of its gruesome details, but is being kept from people so as not to alarm them, and in some cases to cover up their own horrendous culpability.

The era of chemical and biological megadeath is upon us, and the potential of deadly biowarfare attacks from governments, militant independent groups, and even individuals is far greater than it has been at any time in the past. So far the danger of chemical and biological aggression has been little acknowledged, and, at least in America, little prepared for by federal and local governments.

In 1998, American Defense Secretary William Cohen couched a dire warning in semi-cool rhetoric when he spoke of the chemical-biowarfare threat from enemy nation states, criminal organizations, and religious cults. He said, "The front lines are no longer overseas," and added that the threat of a biowarfare attack on the United States is "neither far-fetched nor far off."

The information that is contained in the pages of this book will not be as cool or measured as that voiced by Cohen. It will not be calculated to reassure people that everything is fine, when reassurance is the exact opposite of what is needed at this time. It will not be pretty stuff that we will be confronting, and it may even give you nightmares when you realize the real circumstance that we are in.

The information in the pages that follow will be the truth about the biowarfare threat to America.

# 1

## Hard Facts on Soft War: Biological Weapons

There are three general types of biological weapons: viral, bacteriological, and fungal.

### VIRAL

Viruses are parasitical microorganisms composed of central chromosomes with a surrounding layer of protein. They are normally contracted by human beings through breathing or direct contact, and can otherwise be spread through spraying, spreading through other means, or by exposure to infected animals and insects. Viral agents that can be used in warfare include Lassa fever, Smallpox, Influenza, Marburg fever, Adenovirus, Coxackie virus, Yellow Fever, Dengue fever, Rift Valley fever, and Venezuelan Equine Encephalitis. Possibilities for the use of viral agents in warfare are now relatively open-ended, however, now that genetic engineering is capable of creating wholly new microorganisms whose characteristics in some cases cannot even be imagined.

### BACTERIAL

Bacteria are single-celled microscopic life that in some cases can transform into inactive resistant spores that wait for favorable conditions to multiply. Disease is caused by bacteria through two means:

(a) The invasion of human or animal tissue.

(b) The creation of toxins.

Some bacterials that can be used in biowarfare include Anthrax, the Plague, Cholera, Tularemia, Rickettsias including "Q-fever," Parrot fever, Diptheria, Meningitis, Dysentery, Glanders, Legionnaires' Disease, Tetanus, and

Typhoid fever. Again, with new innovations in genetic engineering, there is no ceiling to the possibilities in the creation of harmful bacterial organisms that can be used for war.

## FUNGAL
Fungi are larger than bacteria or viruses. They are single-celled microorganisms that primarily exist in the form of spores. In warfare, fungi are usually used to infect crops, rather than to produce disease in humans. One by-product of fungi, however, is a wide range of very powerful and resistant poisons, including mycotoxins of the tricothecenes group (used in Soviet "Yellow Rain" biological warfare in Southeast Asia in the '70s and '80s) and aflatoxin, which may have been used by Iraq during the Gulf War. Some fungals that can be used in biowarfare are Valley fever, Histoplasmosis, and Nocardiosis. Again, genetic possibilities for genetic engineering apply.

## TOXINS
Another source of biowarfare weapons are natural toxins derived from a wide variety of sources including snake venom, corals, and shellfish. These toxins include Batrachotoxin, Cobrotoxin, Crotoxin, Ricin, Saxitoxin, and Sea Wasp toxin.

Biological weapons are produced in liquid, powder, and aerosol forms, and can be dispersed in the many ways that these substances can be spread. The possibilities for the dispersion of biological warfare organisms, in fact, are almost endless.

One of the desirable characteristics of using biological weapons in war, according to an expert in the U.S. military, is that "chemical agents will cover only tens of square miles, but biological agents can blanket hundreds of thousands of square miles."

As an example of the potential effectiveness of biological weapons in warfare or terrorist attacks, a recent study by the Office of Technology Assessment reported that the release of about 200 pounds of anthrax bacteria could result in 3 million deaths.

One of the added military advantages to biological weapons is that they can have a delayed effect on their target population. According to one Army manual, "Biological agents are capable of reproducing once they have invaded man. After the microorganisms have multiplied in sufficient quantity, they may overcome the body defenses and cause disease. There is a period of time from the time of entry of microorganisms into man to the time he is actually sick and becomes a casualty. This period of time-to-casualty is specific for each agent and varies from a few days to a few weeks or months."

There are a number of other reasons why biowarfare weapons are so dangerous. Author Leonard A. Cole describes one:

"For many scenarios, a large population cannot be protected against biological attack. Vaccines can prevent some diseases but, unless the causative agent is known in advance, a vaccine may be worthless. Antibiotics are effective against specific bacteria or classes of biological agents, but not against all."

Another factor that makes biological weapons so dangerous is their ready availability. Bioweapons are aptly called "the poor man's atomic bomb" for several reasons. The most obvious is cost. Whereas, the construction of a nuclear bomb might cost hundreds of millions of dollars, building a biological weapon might cost only hundreds of dollars, a figure certainly in the budget range of even the most threadbare terrorist.

In 1969, biological warfare experts spoke before a UN panel. They estimated that, "for a large-scale operation against a civilian population, casualties might cost about $2,000 per square kilometer with conventional weapons, $800 with nuclear weapons, $600 with nerve gas weapons, and $1 with biological weapons."

The dangers of biologicals go even farther. The effects of bioweapons are essentially unpredictable, and such agents can spread far beyond their intended target area. According to Dr. Theodore Rosebury, a BW researcher at Camp Detrick during World War II:

"The horrible potentialities of BW [biological warfare] that the gamesmen and brinksmen seem to enjoy playing with are modified by undertainties they seldom stress. Strategic BW does indeed have enormous possibilities for damage; but it also has a few serious deficiencies. For one thing it is next to impossible to know beforehand what to expect from a strategic BW attack; there is no satisfactory way of testing it in advance."

Another scientist, Dr. Leroy D. Fothergill, wrote in a medical school journal:

"Everything that breathes in the exposed area has an opportunity to be exposed to the agent. This will involve vast numbers of mammals, birds, reptiles, amphibians and insects. Various natural history surveys have indicated surprising numbers of wild life inhabiting each square mile of countryside. It is possible that many species would be exposed to an agent for the first time in their evolutionary history. We have no knowledge of the range of susceptibilities of these many species of wildlife to specific microorganisms, particularly through the respiratory route of administration of infectious aerosols. What would be the consequences? Would new and unused zoonotic foci of endemic disease be established? Would it create the basis for possible genetic evolution of microorganisms in new directions with changes in virulence for some species? Would it create public health and environmental problems that are unique and beyond our present experience?"

These are a few of the many wild cards that one must face when considering biological weaponry.

# 2

## HARD FACTS ON SOFT WAR:
## CHEMICAL WEAPONS

There are several significant classes of chemical weapons agents. For effectiveness, modern chemical weapons are generally delivered in liquid aerosol form, rather than as gases. Some significant classifications of chemical weapons and their military designations are:

### BLISTER AGENTS
These include mustard gas (H) and Lewisite (L), which burn the surface of the body and the respiratory system.

### BLOOD AGENTS
Including hydrogen cyanide (AC) and cyanogen chloride (CK), which enter the body through the respiratory system and attack the blood cells.

### NERVE AGENTS
including the "G" agents tabun, sarin, and soman, and the "V" agents, including VX. The G agents attack through the respiratory system and the skin, while the V agents are absorbed by the skin. Poisoning by nerve agents can be almost instantaneous, death taking place within two or three minutes. Nerve agents act most rapidly through the respiratory system, by binding to and destroying the action of acetylcholinesterase, an enzyme central to the functioning of the human nervous system. They can produce neurological disorders, followed by paralysis, heart and respiratory failure and death.

## INCAPACITATING AGENTS

Incapacitating agents include LSD and more potent psychoactive concoctions such as BZ. These agents, according to the standard text *Military Chemistry and Chemical Agents* (TM 3-215) are of two types:

"(a) Those which produce temporary physical disability such as paralysis, blindness or deafness [psychochemicals]; (b) Those which produce temporary mental aberrations. Unlike the lethal agents, these incapacitants can produce purely temporary effects without permanent damage [anesthetics]."

## HARASSING AGENTS

Another type chemical is the harassing agent, sometimes referred to as "riot control agents." Tear gas, including CN and CS gasses, and pepper spray are examples of same.

# 3

## SPECIAL DELIVERY

There are four general means for the dispersion of biological and chemical warfare agents. These means are through the air, contamination of food or water, contact with infected persons or animals, and by touching objects that have been contaminated.

During wartime, chemicals and biologicals can be sprayed from aircraft, fired in missiles, bombs and artillery projectiles, sprayed by aerosol, or disseminated by explosion or other forms of dispersion.

Initially, the most effective delivery for biological weapons was thought to be air currents, although the invention of bombs, missiles, and aerosol spray tanks on airplanes has largely superceded this belief. Early emphasis was also placed on the use of insects to deliver biowarfare agents, but again, current military thinking on this approach has changed. Although research still takes place in this area, this technique has been replaced with other means of more precise targeting populations.

Water is one effective means of dispersing biological and chemical agents. Reservoirs and central pumping plants are usually not well guarded, and the routine addition of chlorine to water supplies does not proof it against certain chemicals and biologicals. The wartime or terrorist contamination of water supplies is a favorite scenario of experts in biological warfare, and this form of warfare has literally been used for thousands of years.

Another means of dispersing biological agents is through the use of animal disease carriers, such as rats, birds, or insects.

Current emphasis in military applications of CBW weapons is on aerosol dispersion. Military researchers have developed means of stabilization that keep germs virulent after long exposure to air. Historically, one problem with biochemical weapons is that they tend to dissipate so quickly that it limits their effectiveness against targets. This was noted in a 1984 congressional testimony by U.S. Air Force General Charles L. Donnelly, Jr., when describing bombs using sarin: "Two hundred feet away from impact," Donnelly said, "one could virtually hold his breath until it dissipates."

In recent years that problem has been overcome by the technique of microencapsulation, which is similar to timed release medicinal capsules. Using microencapsulation, biochemical agents can released that will persist for years in the environment, or that will release at a set time to target specific groups. They can also be designed so that they are only activated when they land in wet areas such as lakes, streams, or respiratory tracts. The technology can also be employed to deliver sublethal levels of the desired agent for disabling rather than killing soldiers or citizens.

Currently many chemical weapons are kept in what is known as "binary" form. That is, they are composed of two or more chemicals that are combined when used to create the destructive agent. This renders the weapons far more safe during storage or handling than those kept in volatile form.

A truth that is not often mentioned is that America is completely unprepared for a CBW attack from a hostile country or from independent militant factions, and many experts admit that an attack of this nature is almost certain to happen within the next few years. This in essence is the purpose of this book; to alert people to the fact that an attack of this nature is on its way, and to buy them a little time for preparation against such a situation.

There is also the major concern that currently there are no functional early warning or even simple detection methods for biowarfare attack. The most practical method for detecting biological warfare is still by counting the corpses on the deathscape.

As an example of the complete vulnerability of almost all targets to attack, during recent simulated studies, the supposedly safe bunkers underneath the White House and Pentagon command centers have time and again failed simulations of biological warfare attacks. Even nuclear energy facilities, which have been widely criticized for lax security, and installations with high tech security systems are vulnerable, due to the proliferation of information such as *The Barrier Penetration Database* published by the Nuclear Regulatory Commission. This manual, which has circulated clandestinely in revolutionary political circles, includes instructions on breaching sensors and physical barriers, in fact any of thirty-two types of described security barriers, at nuclear power plants.

# 4

## THE BEGINNINGS
## OF BIO-CHEMICAL DEATH

Techniques of chemical and biological warfare weren't born yesterday. The poisoning of wells using disease contaminants has been used as a strategy of war almost since the beginning of recorded history.

An early documented instance occurred in 1346 when the Tartars laid siege to the city of Caffa, on the east coast of the Black Sea. The inhabitants of Caffa were holding their own against the Tartars, we are told, and thought they had won when a plague struck the Tartars. The Italian historian Gabriel de Mussis, describes what followed:

"The Tartars, fatigued by such a plague and pestiferous disease, stupefied and amazed, observing themselves without hope of health, ordered cadavers placed on their hurling machine and thrown into the city of Caffa, so that by means of these intolerable passengers the defenders died widely. Thus there were projected mountains of dead, nor could the Christians hide or flee, or be freed from such disaster... And soon all the air was infected and the water poisoned, corrupt and putrefied."

The Italians, "of whom ten survived of one thousand," surrendered the city of Caffa to the Tartars and fled to Europe, spreading the plague in their path as they went.

In 1456 Belgrade successfully defended itself against the attacking Turks by the invention of an alchemist who prepared a poisonous concoction of unspecified character. Rags were saturated and set afire, producing clouds of poisonous smoke that routed the Turks.

Beginning in 1763 with the British, whole tribes of American Indians were decimated by the distribution of gifts of smallpox-ridden blankets. The U.S. Indian Agency is known to have later used the same strategy against the indigenous peoples of North America.

In America during the Civil War it was a common practice to pollute wells, streams, and water holes when a military force vacated the area. As an example, in July 1863, General Johnston in his retreat from Vicksburg ordered that water sources be poisoned with the decaying bodies of pigs and sheep.

During the Boer War of 1899-1902 in southern Africa, the British fired artillery shells loaded with picric acid.

In 1915 it was claimed that German agents had inoculated horses and cattle with disease organisms as they departed from American ports. Other inoculations are said to have taken place at Bucharest, Romania in 1916, and on the French front in 1917, where 4,500 donkeys were infected with glanders.

In January, 1915, on the Russian Front, German forces unsuccessfully used xylol bromide, which causes irritation of the eyes. Later, the Germans were in a stalemate with French and Algerian troops near Ypres, Belgium. Tear gas had been used by both sides to attempt to rout their opponents, but on April 22, the Germans released from 6,000 cylinders nearly two hundred tons of liquid chlorine, causing a five-foot high cloud of poisonous greenish-yellow gas to drift on a light wind across the trenches to the Allied side.

The action of chlorine gas is not to suffocate; it poisons, creating inflammation that blocks the windpipe and fills the lungs with fluid. A British casualty report stated that each soldier was "being drowned in his own exudation." Another report stated that the victims were in "agony unspeakable, their faces plum colored, while they coughed blood from their tortured lungs."

Over 5,000 Allied troops were killed on the four-mile front, with another 10,000 troops seriously wounded, and a breach was opened in the front lines allowing the Germans to push through.

Two days later the German troops again used chlorine gas, this time against Canadian troops. The Canadians had been given pieces of cloth, to be dipped into urine or bicarbonate of soda, to use as a gas mask. The tactic worked, and although there were casualties, the Canadian line held.

By September 1915, the British were playing turnabout on the Germans, launching gas attacks in Belgium. One major drawback of poison gas was illustrated when the wind shifted, and 2,400 British troops were injured by their own gas attack.

The strategy of using poisonous gas in warfare continued to escalate, with a total of about fifty types of poison gas used during World War I. Thirty-three British laboratories were engaged in the research of chemical and gas warfare during this period.

In 1916 the British opened a large chemical warfare facility at Porton Down, on Salisbury Plain. The installation employed over a thousand scientists and soldiers laboring to research and produce chemical weapons.

In April of 1917 the British launched the first attack against the Germans using a new invention called the Livens Projector. The Projector was a steel tube, usually built up in banks of twenty-five at a time, that fired a thirty-pound drum usually containing phosgene. The phosgene drums would explode, raining down poisonous gas over the heads of German troops. At the Battle of Arras 2,340 of these projectiles were fired.

In July of 1917 the Germans used a new tactic to counter the British, firing artillery shells charged with mustard gas. The mustard gas had a delayed effect, and many Allied soldiers thought that they were safe, and removed their gas masks. Within hours they were suffering the effects of the gas, and within three weeks there were 15,000 British casualties. By 1918 almost as many artillery shells carried gas as explosives. By the end of World War I, an estimated 66 million gas shells had been fired, and 800,000 soldiers had died from poison gas attacks, according to the Encyclopedia Britannica.

In 1917 the U.S. military constructed Edgewood Arsenal. This 10,000 acre location fifteen miles northeast of Baltimore, Maryland remains to this day the management center for American chemical weaponry. Edgewood was initially used for the manufacture and loading of poison gas artillery shells to be used in World War I, but the location continued to be the central manufacturing facility for the Army Chemical Corps until the end of World War II. At that point the purpose of the facility was altered: now it primarily specializes in research and development, although a plant for the production of sarin nerve agent was operating on the base as of the late 1940s.

Edgewood Arsenal was the first American facility to experiment with chemical warfare agents on humans, specifically U.S. Army volunteers. [Hersh]

In 1966 officers at the base reported that a nearby river had been contaminated through waste disposal from the arsenal. Although such figures are notoriously unreliable, given that the military is not anxious to advertise its mistakes, the Army reports that there have been 464 illnesses and one death attributable to chemical warfare research at Edgewood since 1950. This is almost certainly an underestimate.

In early 1919 the British intervened in the Russian civil war with the 'M' device, a canister that spewed out clouds of arsenic smoke. Later in the year the British used phosgene and mustard gas against tribesmen near the Afghan frontier. By 1925 the French and Spanish were using gas warfare in Morocco.

After the war, in 1925, a conference on international arms trade was convened in Geneva. On June 17 the Geneva Protocol was written, with 38 nations originally signing the document, followed by almost 100 others as the years went by. The document states,

"The undersigned Plenipotentiaries, in the name of their respective governments:

"Whereas the use in war of asphyxiating, poisonous or other gases, and of all analogous liquids, materials or devices, has been justly condemned by the general opinion of the civilized world; and:

"Whereas the prohibition of such use has been declared in Treaties to which the majority of Powers of the world are Parties; and:

"To the end that this prohibition shall be universally accepted as a part of International Law, binding alike the conscience and practice of nations;

"Declare:

"That the High Contracting Parties, so far as they are not already Parties to Treaties prohibiting such use, accept this prohibition, agree to extend this prohibition to the use of bacteriological methods of warfare and agree to be bound as between themselves according to the terms of this declaration..."

Signing the Protocol, however, was not enough. Each signatory also had to ratify the document. France ratified first, in 1926; Italy and the Soviet Union ratified in 1928; Germany did so in 1929; and Britain ratified in 1930. Some lagged behind. Japan did not ratify until 1970; America held back until 1975.

Although the Geneva Protocol remains to this day the most effective constraint against chemical and biological warfare, like many other accords, it has proven to be made only of paper. Numerous countries have already violated the pact and it is no secret that the first and overriding creed of political entities in war is the law of the jungle.

The agreement by most of the world's governments not to initiate the use of poison gas in warfare did nothing to stop research and stockpiling, it simply compelled greater secrecy for those who were doing it. Research into chemical weapons in Britain actually increased after the signing of the Protocol, with 3,000 tons of mustard gas being produced per week by 1938.

The Russians and the Germans began 'Project Tomka" near Volsk in the Soviet Union, primarily engaged in the testing of mustard gas.

Production of mustard gas in Japan began in 1928, with research escalating until the country possessed a wide array and huge stockpile of chemical weapons. Japanese biowarfare experimentation also began in 1931. In 1936 two facilities dedicated to biological production were built in Manchuria. Among the weapons that were cultured were cholera, plague, salmonella, typhus, typhoid, anthrax, tetanus, tuberculosis, tularemia, glanders, botulism, brucellosis, gas gangrene, smallpox, and tick encephalitis.

The Russians estimated the production capacity of one of the Manchurian facilities at eight tons of bacterial cultures per month.

Between 1937 and 1945, the Japanese used poison gas and germ warfare against soldiers and civilians during the invasion of China, dumping these agents on eleven Chinese cities. Japanese biological weaponry included the *Uji* and *Ha* fragmentation bombs, which burst into tiny anthrax spore-coated splinters. Lethality is reported to have exceeded 90% in those even scratched by one of the splinters.

According to a British journalist, Wickham Steed, in 1931 there was a German plot to release Serratia marcescens bacteria into the underground railways of London and Paris. Apparently the Germans were thwarted in the plan.

During World War II, according to a published report of the Institute of Medicine, about 60,000 American servicemen were used in the testing of mustard gas and lewisite. Most of these men were not informed of the nature of the tests they would be undergoing, and did not receive medical attention after being exposed to these agents. Some of the men were threatened with imprisonment if they discussed the experiments with anyone, including their family doctors. The Pentagon for decades denied that testing of this nature had taken place, allowing the Veterans' Administration to deny claims for compensation, in a grim precursor to their behavior after the Gulf War.

A particularly horrible incident took place in 1931, and is to be laid on the table of American researchers. The Puerto Rican Cancer Experiment, run by the Rockefeller Institute for Medical Investigations, under the direction of Dr. Cornelius Rhoads, purposely infected thirteen Puerto Ricans with cancer. Rhoads wrote:

"The Porto Ricans [sic]... are beyond doubt the dirtiest, laziest, most degenerate and thievish race of men ever inhabiting this sphere. It makes you sick to inhabit the same island with them... What the island needs is not public health work, but a tidal wave or something to totally exterminate the population. It might then be livable. I have done my best to further the process of extermination by killing off eight and transplanting cancer into several more. The latter has not resulted in any fatalities so far... The matter of consideration for the patients' welfare plays no role here — in fact, all physicians take delight in the abuse and torture of the unfortunate subjects."

Far from being prosecuted for his crimes, Dr. Rhoads was awarded the Legion of Merit by the U.S. government, and then appointed to the U.S. Atomic Energy Commission.

In 1935, the Japanese military police, the *Kempai*, arrested five Russians thought to be spies in Kwangtung in China. The Russians were said to be carrying bottles of anthrax, cholera, and dysentery. Apparently the Russians had already been hard at work using some of the germ weapons; 6,000 Japanese soldiers died from cholera in Shanghai, and 2,000 army horses died from anthrax infection.

In 1935 and 1936, the Italian air force used mustard gas, delivered both in spray and in bombs, against Abyssinian troops and civilians. Around 15,000 troops were killed by gas in the war. Abyssinian Emperor Haile Selassie, in a speech to the League of Nations, told how "groups of nine, fifteen and eighteen aircraft followed one another so that the liquid issuing from them formed a continuous fog... soldiers, women, children, cattle, rivers, lakes and pastures were drenched continually with this deadly rain."

In 1936 Dr. Gerhard Schrader, working in Germany for the munitions conglomerate I.G. Farben discovered tabun, the first nerve gas, and the most virulent chemical for warfare that had then been discovered.

Nerve gases inhibit a chemical in the body called cholinesterase, whose function is to control the muscles. The inhibition of this chemical causes the contraction of all of the muscles in the body, resulting in asphyxiation. Nerve agents are colorless and odorless, and when inhaled or absorbed through the skin they block transmission of nerve impulses, causing wild convulsions and death through suffocation. Even the tiniest amount of tabun, it was found, would kill whatever animal was exposed to it.

In September of 1939 work began on a secret factory in western Poland at Dyhernfurth with the capacity achieved in 1942 to produce 3,000 tons of nerve gas per month. There were at least 300 accidents involving nerve gas at Dyhernfurth. One scientist who worked there recalled an incident where liquid tabun drained on to pipefitters as they were cleaning pipes. "These workmen died in convulsions before the rubber suits could be torn off." One man had half a gallon of tabun drained down his neck; he died in two minutes.

In the next few years the Germans would discover sarin (about ten times as lethal as tabun) and soman, more toxic than either tabun or sarin. By 1945, they had produced about 250,000 tons of nerve agents, according to British and American estimates, with the major nerve agent stockpiled being tabun.

A wide variety of weapons were devised by the Germans using nerve gas, including artillery shells and missiles laden with the chemicals. Nerve agents were tested on inmates of concentration camps, and persons who were sentenced to death were sometimes dispatched with bullets poisoned with aconitine, a chemical closely related to the nerve gases.

When the tabun factory at Dyhrenfurth near Breslau was overrun by the Russians, there were 12,000 pounds of tabun discovered there. The Russians confiscated the tabun, and it is reported that they later took the whole factory and moved it to the Urals, where it resumed production of nerve agents.

It is thought that the reason that the Germans did not use their massive stockpiles of nerve agents on the Allies was because Hitler himself had been injured with mustard gas in World War I, and had a particular aversion to that form of warfare. As Germany went down in defeat Nazi leaders Bormann, Goebbels and Ley urged Hitler to use nerve gas on the Allies. Hitler rejected this idea, but speculated that he might use it against the Soviets without retaliation, because the British and Americans were also interested in stopping the Russian advance. Ultimately, the reason that Hitler failed to order the use of nerve gas was probably his conviction that the Allies also possessed such agents, and would be quick to retaliate with them. In fact, they did not.

The entry of the United States into biowarfare testing happened in 1941 with the urging of Secretary of War Henry Stimson, who said, in a letter to Dr. Frank B. Jewett, then president of the National Academy of Sciences, "Because of the dangers that might confront this country from potential enemies employing what may be broadly described as biological warfare, it seems advisable that investigations be initiated to survey the present situation and the future possibilities. I am therefore, asking if you will undertake the appointment of an appropriate committee to survey all phases of this matter. Your organization already has before it a request from The Surgeon General for the appointment of a committee by the Division of Medical sciences of the National Research Council to examine one phase of the matter. I trust that appropriate integration of these efforts can be arranged."

A few months later Stimson was authorized by President Roosevelt to develop a civilian agency on biological warfare. The group functioned out of the Federal Security Agency, and was headed by George Merck of the War Research Service. Merck's name later become ubiquitous in the American biowarfare industry, as well as in the commercial manufacture of pharmaceuticals.

After authorization by Roosevelt, American biological warfare research took place at four locations:

Camp Detrick, in Maryland (known as 'The Health Farm') employed approximately 5,000 workers and scientists. Camp Detrick would be the major location for biowarfare research in the years to come. A wide variety of research has taken place there, including the development of dozens of bacterial and viral organisms and the weapons that would be used to deliver them.

The Field Testing Station at Horn Island, Pascagoula, Mississippi.

A production plant at Vigo, near Terre Haute, Indiana. This facility employed around 500 persons, and was the main production center for biological bombs.

The Field Testing Station near Dugway, Utah, where for many years germ bombs were exploded in the open air. Among the germ agents used at Dugway were Q-fever, anthrax, San Joaquin Valley Fever, Venezuelan equine encephalitis, brucellosis, tularemia, and plague.

Between 1942 to 1945, the United States also opened thirteen new industrial plants designed for the production of chemical weapons.

In 1941 British and American scientists launched a secret project for the development of anthrax as a biowarfare weapon. This research was done on Gruinard Island, off the coast of Scotland. Although it was assumed that the island would safely contain any anthrax spores that were released from bombs detonated there, this was not the case. Concurrent with the testing, anthrax broke out on the mainland of Scotland.

Another effect of the testing was that the island was permanently contaminated with disease organisms, despite the fact that the scientists had reassured the government that this would not happen. On Gruinard, the rabbits have turned black as they have mutated into immunity from the anthrax spores.

Warning signs are still in place on Gruinard Island:

THIS ISLAND IS GOVERNMENT PROPERTY UNDER EXPERIMENT. THE GROUND IS CONTAMINATED WITH ANTHRAX AND DANGEROUS LANDING IS PROHIBITED.

In 1941, in response to a proposal by the 'Sub-Committee' at Porton Downs, Winston Churchill authorized the production of five million large pellets infected with anthrax to be used against cattle and humans in Germany.

By 1943, the Americans, collaborating with the British had developed the first biological bomb, code named 'N,' containing anthrax spores. In May of 1944 an initial 5,000 anthrax bombs rolled off the production line at Camp Detrick, and within two months production of the bombs was taken over by an undisclosed factory with a higher capacity for production.

Other bombs of the same kind were later fashioned using botulism toxin. The United States also developed germ weapons for use against plant crops, with the intended target being the rice fields of Japan.

In December of 1942 a germ warfare stockpile was discovered by the Gestapo in a Polish underground safehouse in Warsaw. According to a report to Himmler, they found "three flasks of typhus bacilli, seventeen sealed rubber tubes presumably containing bacteria, and one fountain pen with instructions for use for spreading bacteria." There were also 20 pounds of arsenic stockpiled in the house.

It was claimed by a Russian deserter named Von Apen that in 1941 germ warfare experiments using humans were carried out by the Soviets in Mongolia. The victims are said to have been political prisoners and Japanese prisoners of war, and they were infected with plague, anthrax, and glanders. Supporting the man's contention, an epidemic began in the area, and about 5,000 Mongols died.

In November of 1944, the Mufti of Jerusalem and German Nazis were engaged in a plot to poison the wells of Tel Aviv. Police discovered ten containers of poison cached in a safehouse, each of them containing enough poison to kill an estimated ten thousand persons.

At the end of World War II the Russians captured twelve Japanese biological laboratories and notified the U.S. that the Japanese had been engaging in biological weapons testing using humans. At least 3,000 American, Chinese, Korean, Australian, and Russian prisoners of war died from the experiments. The Americans also captured Japanese chemical-biological warfare scientists, many of whom had participated in murderous experimentation against American prisoners of war.

During the Khabarovsk War Crimes Trial in 1947 one witness reported, "Ten prisoners were tied facing stakes, five to ten meters apart... The prisoners' heads were covered with metal helmets and their bodies with screens... [with]

only the naked buttocks being exposed... a fragmentation bomb was exploded... all ten men were wounded... They told me all ten men had... died of gas gangrene."

The experiments the Japanese conducted were as horrific as any attributed to the Nazis, but the Americans saw the potential of utilizing their research and offered them immunity from prosecution in exchange for their participation in American programs.

According to a report of the State, War, Navy Coordinating Committee for the Far East on August 1, 1947, "The value to the US of Japanese BW [biowarfare] data is of such importance to national security as to far outweigh the value accruing for 'war crimes' prosecution."

The report also noted that, "It should be kept in mind that there is a remote possibility that investigation conducted by the Soviets in the Mukden area may have disclosed evidence that American prisoners of war were used for experimental purposes of a BW nature and that they lost their lives as a result of these experiments."

Not only did the American military protect Japanese scientists who had participated in biological warfare experiments that had resulted in the death of American soldiers, in a move that foreshadowed later government cover-ups, the Army denied that there had ever been such experiments. Despite the reports of many American prisoners of war in Japanese internment camps, spokesmen for the Army denied that documentation existed to prove that these programs had ever existed.

At the close of World War II many Nazi scientists escaped prosecution by being brought to the United States by the military, to work in their own projects. According to researcher Peter Dale Scott, Walter Schreiber, a colleague of Mengele at Auschwitz, was saved from prosecution in Poland and participated in biowarfare research under the auspices of the U.S. Air Force. Nazi biological warfare expert Erich Traub and his assistant Anne Burger began work for the Navy in 1951 at the Naval Medical Research Institute laboratory in Bethesda. Traub was given the task of experimentation on animals to determine the lethal doses of forty dangerous viruses.

During World War II the world barely escaped the major use of biological and chemical warfare. It is said that Japan escaped gas attacks by the United States only through the personal intervention of President Roosevelt in the closing days of the war. Either through civility or fear of retribution these weapons were not used extensively, and the invention of the atomic bomb seemed to render the whole matter moot: at least for a while. That view was not to persist for long. With the Cold War a new era in biochemical warfare began.

# 5

## LAND OF THE FREE
## HOME OF THE DEAD

In response to growing concerns about the power of the Soviet Union, in 1948 the Research and Development Board of the office of the Secretary of Defense requested an assessment of biological weapons, and the Committee on Biological Warfare was brought into being. On October 5, the committee issued a report that was used as the justification for the launching of the Special Operations Division, as well as for open air testing and covert testing of CBW agents on the American populace.

### FORT DETRICK

The Special Operations Division was housed in a one-story cinderblock building at Fort Detrick in Maryland. This facility would evolve into the management center for America's program of biological weaponry and defense systems. Fort Detrick was so secret that even generals inspecting the base would bypass the SOD headquarters.

SOD liaised with the CIA, and worked with many of the same personnel, including prominent MKULTRA mind control researchers Stanley Lovell and Sidney Gottlieb. Fort Detrick's purpose as a research station for germ warfare was not officially acknowledged until after World War II. According to Ira Baldwin, Camp Detrick's first technical director, "The only agency that had more priority than we had, if one hadn't a uniform on and was in this country, was the Manhattan Project."

Fort Detrick has continued to use human subjects for testing germ agents after the end of World War II. There are numerous reasons to feel uneasy about the use of volunteers involved in these tests. As an example, in 1967, the

*New York Times Magazine* reported that 585 Air Force volunteers who had contracted food poisoning were treated with sulfa instead of penicillin in order to discover the effectiveness of the sulfa. Twenty-five of the volunteers developed rheumatic fever in this experiment hearkening to the kind of callousness towards research subjects that was exhibited in the Nazi era.

The article stated:

"Medical officers involved in the experiment admit that those 25 patients were given no real idea of the risks to which they were being subjected. They had a right to assume that they were receiving the best care available for their infections. In any case, even if the doctors had told the test group the whole story, even if each airman's consent had been asked, and given, the situation would have been suspect because of the military status of patients... Soldiers, like prisoners hoping for parole, welfare cases hoping for attention, students hoping for good marks, are favorite subjects of experimentation."

The Army admits that between 1943 and 1969 workers at Fort Detrick were accidentally infected 423 times by organisms used as biowarfare weapons. Two of the most prevalent infections amongst the victims were Q-fever and tularemia. One wonders, however, about the reliability of these figures, given incidents such as those which will follow.

### ROCKY MOUNTAIN ARSENAL

In the early 1950s Rocky Mountain Arsenal, a 17,750 acre base located near Denver, Colorado, began producing and storing thousands of gallons of nerve gas of various types. Hundreds of thousands of bombs and rockets have been armed with nerve agents at this base. These chemicals are stored in the open in steel garbage can-like containers. The area is under 24-hour surveillance, with chemical containers electrically grounded in case of lightning strikes.

In 1954, Lieutenant Colonel S.J. Efnor, in an interview with the *Rocky Mountain News*, said that, "The gas from a single bomb the size of a quart fruit jar could kill every living thing within a cubic mile, depending on the wind and weather conditions... A tiny drop of the gas in its liquid form on the back of a man's hand will paralyze his nerves instantly and deaden his brain in a few seconds. Death will follow in 30 second."

Statements like this have caused some to ponder the wisdom of storing all of that nerve gas in the open.

Since 1960 there have been about 1,800 industrial accidents at Rocky Mountain Arsenal, and although the Army Industrial Fund that runs the Arsenal denies that any deaths have taken place, this may be a cover-up. We have documentation on at least one case of a worker at the facility who died from exposure to either sarin or to the insecticide parathion.

One of the problems with chemical and biological weapons has always been that of disposal. During the 1950s the facility dumped waste products, mostly contaminated salts we are told, into landfill on the property. In the early and mid-1950s farmers in an approximate six-mile area surrounding the arsenal were complaining of crop and stock losses from contamination. Their conclusions were backed up by chemical tests showing that the ground water was contaminated with chemicals from the arsenal. Studies also showed that approximately 2,000 ducks and other waterfowl were dying from drinking from the arsenal's sewage. No reports are available on a possible increase in the incidence of diseases amongst the human population in surrounding areas.

### DUGWAY PROVING GROUND

Another hot spot of biological and chemical warfare testing in the United States has been Dugway Proving Ground, about 70 miles southwest of Salt Lake City. Dugway, composed of an area 50 miles wide and 30 miles long, has been in operation since 1942. Among other testing taking place at this location, there have been over one thousand open air sprayings of bacteria and chemicals.

Although the Army considers Dugway a safe location for testing these sorts of weapons, there are small towns and Indian reservations located within 20 miles of the facility that are at great risk from the testing. There are also approximately 10,000 vehicles driving by Dugway on a daily basis. There have been numerous accidents at Dugway that will be documented later.

Beginning in 1948, major tests of biowarfare were jointly conducted by the British, Canadians and Americans, in the Bahamas. This was not an unusual tack, since by the end of World War II the chemical and biowarfare programs of these countries were almost seamlessly integrated.

In 1948 Operation Harness was launched, with Operations Ozone and Negation taking place in 1953 and 1954. Thousands of animals were tethered on rafts at sea, and "highly virulent organisms," believed to have included anthrax, brucellosis, and tularemia were sprayed, killing all of the animals.

It is probable that some of the infective agents drifted to shore, since Dr. R.G.H. Watson, director of the British Chemical Defense Establishment stated in 1981 that "major animal species" on the islands died during the tests, including guinea pigs, mice, monkeys, and rabbits.

Then the testing moved to the United States. From the middle of this century to 1969, the U.S. military is documented as having exposed millions of persons in the United States to a variety of germ and chemical agents in over three hundred tests in the United States. Testing took place throughout the United States and Canada, and there were specific bombardments of many forts, schools, Air Force bases, and test stations.

During the early 1950s the army experimented with biowarfare agents targeted for the destruction of livestock and plant life. At Eglin Air Force Base in Florida they exploded feather bombs infected with hog cholera over pigpens, and dropped Newcastle disease over University of Washington chicken farms. They tested defoliants and crop killing weapons widely in the United States, using simulants and actual crop killing agents.

The military has always insisted that in tests using civilians it used simulant agents, "considered by the scientific community to be totally safe." The Army, for one, knows that this is not true, as proved by materials submitted to Senate subcommittee hearings in 1977 admitting that some of the agents used in open air testing were not entirely safe. As is so often the case, there was no after-the-fact monitoring of the health of persons exposed to these programs, and so in most cases any detrimental effects on the populace can only be speculated about.

The four most common simulants used in the United States in military tests are:

Aspergillus Fumigatus is a fungus that the Army sprayed widely over populated areas in the U.S in the 1950s. This agent is known to cause aspergillosis, which in turn causes pulmonary and generalized infections, "which frequently are fatal."

Bacillus subtilis has been commonly used by the military in simulated biowarfare attacks, including spraying over American cities and continued outdoor spraying at Dugway Proving Ground in Utah. This is because this bacteria shares characteristics with Bacillus anthracis, a biowarfare agent that causes anthrax. Although the Army contends that Bacillus subtilis is harmless, standard medical texts do not concur with this opinion. According to one such text, the agent causes "infections in man; pulmonary and disseminated infections in immunologically compromised hosts; localized infections in a closed space (e.g. opthalmitis, meningitis); wound infections following trauma, surgery, or the introduction of foreign prosthetic material."

Serratia Marcescens was used for at least twenty years in sprayings in the United States, and during that period serratia infections became increasingly common and were acknowledged for the first time "as a cause of serious infection in man." A study was released in the early 1950s indicating that the bacterium caused meningitis, wound infection, and arthritis. This agent was reportedly taken out of use as a simulant by the U.S. military in the 1970s.

Zinc cadmium sulfide is a fluorescent powder that has been sprayed by itself and sometimes in combination with bacteriological agents.

According to an Army report on 239 biological warfare tests that it had conducted, zinc cadmium sulfide has been used in 34 open air tests, although verified evidence has shown that there have been other sprayings of the chemical not mentioned in the Army report. Zinc cadmium sulfide has long been acknowledged to be dangerous to humans, and according to L. Arthur Spomer, a professor in the School of Agriculture at the University of Illinois, the chemical is "toxic to almost all physiological systems." Spomer wrote,

"Although Cd (cadmium) toxicity is well-established and FP (flourescent particles) is commonly used as a tracer in atmospheric studies, no case of Cd poisoning resulting from the use of FP has been reported in the literature. This may be because none has occurred; however, it is more likely that such poisoning has been of a low-level chronic nature and its symptoms are less dramatic and more difficult to recognize than in the case of acute Cd poisoning."

According Army spokespersons, zinc cadmium sulfide was retired as a simulant during the 1970s.

Although the details of many of these tests are still classified, there is information available on some of them.

At least six simulated biowarfare tests were conducted in the San Francisco Bay area in September 20-27, 1950. Bacillus globigii and Serratia marcescens bacteria as well as zinc cadmium sulfide was disseminated via aerosol from a ship slowly travelling along the shoreline. According to Army reports, nearly everyone in San Francisco inhaled the particles. An epidemic of Serratia marcescens infections took place in San Francisco immediately following the testing.

A 1976 report by John Mills, a professor at the University of California Medical Center in San Francisco, indicated that Serratia marcescens infections in the San Francisco Bay area were five to ten times as frequent as in other locations. Mills wondered if tests by the Army "could have seeded the Bay area environment."

In 1952 an investigation was launched by the International Scientific Commission to look into allegations that the United States had dropped biological warfare weapons from airplanes in China and North Korea. Six internationally recognized scientists visited the areas where attacks had been made, and heard witnesses describe over-flys of American planes that dropped insects and animal life infected with anthrax and cholera, along with information on subsequent disease outbreaks that took place. The U.S. Army denied the allegations, as do most of the apologists for the military who see fit to write books on biowarfare.

The truth is that the U.S. probably did use biowarfare weapons during the Korean War. The Army has admitted that biological weapons were produced for the conflict, and a top secret memo refers to a "Cover and Deception Plan for Biological Warfare" named Plan Schoolyard that was approved by the military.

Reports in the *New York Times* at the time told about the U.S. Army setting up a bacteriological weapons research lab in Japan, run by World War II Japanese biowarfare experts, and *Newsweek* and Associated Press reported a "Navy epidemic control laboratory" cruising the coast of North Korea, also at precisely the time of the alleged attacks. This may have been the same vessel described by two U.S. officials requesting anonymity who reported that General Ridgeway had sent Shro Ishii, Jiro Wakamatsu, and Masajo Kitano, infamous Japanese biowarfare specialists, to Korea with a seagoing freighter "carrying all the necessary equipment."

William Powell, editor of the English-language *China Monthly Review* wrote, "Proceeding in a vein which surpasses the savagery of Hitler Germany and Hirohito Japan in the last war, the American invaders, by a systematic spreading of smallpox, cholera and plague germs over North Korea have shocked and horrified the entire world. Since VJ Day, Japanese war criminals turned into 'experts' have been working for the Americans in developing bacteriological warfare."

Powell reported that American aircraft had dropped "special paper and cardboard containers filled with various types of flies, fleas, ticks, spiders, mosquitoes and other bacteria-carrying insects" in February and March of 1952.

For his trouble, Powell was charged with sedition by the U.S. government, but a lengthy trial and investigation was ordered dropped by President Kennedy in 1961.

In the first three months of 1953, zinc cadmium sulfide, a fluorescent powder meant to simulate bacterial agents, was sprayed by the Army from blower-type generators in sixty-one locations in Minneapolis, Minnesota. According to the Army, the Minneapolis tests "are part of a continuing program designed to provide the field experimental data necessary to estimate munitions requirements for the strategic use of chemical and biological agents against typical target cities." The Army afterward noted respiratory problems among some persons exposed to the chemical.

One of the areas that was targeted for the spraying of the zinc cadmium sulfide was the Clinton elementary school. Hundreds of former students of the school now report that they are suffering illnesses which they attribute to exposure to the chemical.

The Minneapolis tests were duplicated in St. Louis, Missouri, in April through June of 1953. Zinc cadmium sulfide was sprayed in thirty-five locations during these tests.

In 1955 the CIA conducted studies on the populace of the Gulf Coast of Florida, using whooping cough germs. The number of cases of whooping cough in the area tripled during that period, with approximately 350 deaths from the disease occurring.

"Operation CD 22" or "Operation Whitecoat" were a series of biowarfare experiments beginning in 1955 and lasting for several years. The tests were conducted by the Army "to effect the exposure of human test subjects to a typical BW [biological warfare] aerosol." Rickettsia burnetii germs were released from generators at Dugway Proving Ground, spraying guinea pigs, monkeys, and humans. Rickettsia is the cause of Q fever, and causes fever, vomiting, and pneumonitis. Although the disease is not often fatal, relapses of varying severity can occur during the course of the life of a person who has been infected.

From 1956 to 1958 the Army released mosquitoes from airplanes and helicopters into poor black residential areas of Savannah, Georgia and Avon Park Florida. Some persons in the area developed fevers of an unknown type. After each of the several tests conducted, Army agents entered the areas. Posing as health officials they ran tests and took photos of victims. Researchers have speculated that the mosquitoes dropped by the Army may have been infected with yellow fever.

Beginning in 1957, the Army Chemical Corps conducted a series of tests termed "Operation LAC," again using the toxic and potentially carcinogenic chemical zinc cadmium sulfide. The scope of the tests is described in the *Summary of Major Events and Problems* published by the Corps:

"Operation LAC, which received its name from the initials of the words, "Large Area Coverage," was the largest test ever undertaken by the Chemical Corps. The test area covered the United States from the Rockies to the Atlantic, from Canada to the Gulf of Mexico. In brief, the Corps dropped a myriad of microscopic particles from a plane, and determined the distance and direction these particles traveled with the wind. The Corps wanted to learn these things: would it be feasible to contaminate a large area by this method using, for example BW [biological warfare] organisms, and if so, what logistics would be involved.

"The first test took place on 2 December 1957. A C119 "flying boxcar," loaned to the Corps by the Air Force, flew along a path leading from South Dakota to International Falls, Minnesota, dispersing fluorescent particles of zinc cadmium sulfide into the air. A large mass of cold air moving down from Canada carried particles along. Meteorologists expected the air mass to continue south across the United States, but instead it turned and went northeast, carrying the bulk of the material into Canada. The test was incomplete, but it was partially successful since some stations 1200 miles away in New York State detected the particles."

Additional Operation LAC tests were conducted. According to the same report:

"Dugway [Proving Ground in Utah] ran a second trial in February 1958. This time the "polar outbreak," as the Canadian cold air masses are generally called, continued on to the Gulf of Mexico, carrying fluorescent particles with it. As the air mass moved south the front broadened so that the line of particles 200 miles long at the aircraft's path spread out to 600 miles at the Gulf...

"During the spring of 1958 Dugway conducted two additional tests, this time with the wind blowing haphazardly instead of steady [sic] from the north. In the first, the plane flew from Toledo, Ohio, and then turned west to Abilene, Texas. In the second, the course ran from Detroit to Springfield, Illinois, then west to Goodland, Kansas. Sampling stations on both sides of the flight path reported particles, proving that random flight over a target area would disperse small particles widely."

Areas that were covered by the dispersion of at least 5,000 pounds of zinc cadmium sulfide particles included Ohio, Indiana, Illinois, Kentucky, Arkansas, Oklahoma, Louisiana, and Texas, with the later test Michigan, Illinois, and Kansas. But wind-borne dispersion of the particles is acknowledged to have covered most of the United States.

In 1958 construction on state-of-the-art research laboratories commenced at Fort Detrick known as Special Operations X (XO-X) labs. These laboratories may have also been designed for early research into genetics for biowarfare.

On June 28, 1958, Joel Willard, a civilian carpenter working at Fort Detrick, entered an unsecured laboratory to change light bulbs. The following day he became ill, and he died on July 6. For unspecified reasons which are not difficult to imagine, he was buried within 36 hours after his death. When the local Frederick *News-Post* reported Willard's death, he was said to have died "of an occupational illness which was described by a Fort Detrick official as a respiratory disease." His death certificate provided the real cause of death: myocardial failure from visceral anthrax.

Throughout the 1950s and 1960s, the Department of Defense and the CIA dosed thousands of servicemen with hallucinogenic drugs, including LSD and BZ. The servicemen were often not informed of the nature of the experimentation that would be done upon them.

In 1960 the chief of Army research, Major General Marshall Stubbs, claimed that the Soviets were far ahead of the Americans in terms of germ and chemical warfare. He told of the grave threat of biological weapons and said that an enemy could kill or seriously disable 30 percent of the American population with an attack mounted by as few as ten aircraft. Unlike many false alarms that have been issued by the military in order to obtain increased funding, the general's dire warning was absolutely true.

Congress did not, however, do the logical thing, which would have been to devise means to protect the public from such an attack. Instead, alarmed, they authorized increased spending in offensive biological and chemical weapons research. The budget for U.S. research and development of such weapons, funneled to the military and at least three hundred private companies, was gradually boosted from about $10 million per year to $352 million per year by 1969.

In the early 1960s the Army sought ways to spread smallpox effectively, using covert agents at Washington's National Airport. The agents set up briefcases with mini-generators that shot simulant bacterial agents into the air, with other agents following behind, taking air samples.

Due to the complaints of the farmers and other citizens, in 1960 scientists at Rocky Mountain Arsenal decided to change their approach and to dump 165,000,000 gallons of toxic waste into an underground cavern instead of simply burying it as they had been doing until that time. This was enough toxic waste to fill a fifty-acre lake to a depth of ten feet. After five years of dumping, 1,500 earth tremors in the area made the scientists wonder if that had been such a good idea.

A 1966 study by the Colorado School of Mines came to the conclusion that earthquakes had increased as more waste was pumped into the underground well, causing some to draw the conclusion that the pumping had actually stimulated the

earthquakes. The Army announced that they would investi-
gate the idea of pumping the toxic waste back out of the cavern. After lengthy testing, they determined that it would take
over a thousand years to do so, and abandoned the idea.

There have been other unique ways of disposing of chemical waste that have been employed at the Rocky Mountain
Arsenal. In March of 1998 I was contacted by a woman who
had worked as a proofreader on top secret documents origi-
nating from the facility. She told me of one instance where
toxic chemicals in canisters were released from trucks driving in the area, the chemicals simply being dispersed into the
air.

During the Vietnamese War, 'Black Magic' was the code
name for a crash project to manufacture CS gas in large
quantities. CS is an irritant that causes burning eyes and skin,
coughing, vomiting, and difficulty in breathing. Thousands of
tons of CS were sprayed on Vietnam, with the rationale that
the gas would cause the Viet Cong to abandon their bunkers,
therefore being more susceptible to bombing raids. CS is also
the gas that was used on men, women, and children during
the deadly confrontation at the David Koresh compound in
Waco Texas.

In November of 1961, the Americans began 'Operation
Ranch Hand, using chemical defoliants to denude the jungle
in the Cambodian-Laotian-North Vietnamese border and the
Mekong Delta, 31,250 square miles of jungle, thus theoretically depriving the Viet Cong of protective cover. Six chemicals were used during this operation, dubbed Agents Green,
Pink, Purple, White, Blue, and Orange after the colors of the
barrels the chemicals were stored in. By 1964 Ranch Hand
aircraft were dumping their cargos of poison over the whole
of Vietnam.

Agent Orange, used to destroy dense areas of forest, is
the most infamous of the chemical agents used. Areas sprayed
are described as turning into mutated, surrealistic wastelands.
Vietnamese peasants called these areas "The land of the
dead."

Agent Orange is a combination of two chemicals, one of which, 245T, contains dioxin, a chemical known to cause deformities in animal fetuses.

Servicemen say that Agent Orange stripped the paint from airplanes, and doctors at the Saigon Children's Hospital report that during this period babies suffering spinal bifida and cleft palates tripled. The crews of helicopters spraying Agent Orange would sometimes be completely covered by the herbicide, and in over forty instances Agent Orange was accidentally dumped over American military bases.

After the Vietnam War the horrors continued. Although there has not been a formal study done, Vietnamese doctors note a higher incidence of birth defects among children, and a greatly increased amount of liver ailments including cancer among adults.

After the Vietnam War, thousands of American servicemen suffered illnesses such as fatigue, nervous disorders, and cancer, due, they believed, to the effects of Agent Orange. Although the government was conveniently protected from a law suit, the servicemen did enact a class action suit against seven chemical companies that had manufactured Agent Orange. In 1984, the companies settled out of court for $180 million.

In 1962, as part of a covert attack against communist Cuba, a Canadian agricultural technician was paid $5,000 and provided with a vial of Newcastle virus to infect turkeys on the island. The technician threw the vial away, but eight thousand turkeys on the island died anyway. Newcastle virus, as it turns out, was a biowarfare agent that the Army had experimented with in the past. The strong probability is that another saboteur was successful in carrying out the mission.

In 1965 $1.3 million was appropriated by Congress in order to correct unspecified problems at the viral and rickettsial lab at Fort Detrick, referred to as Building 539. Dr. Arthur N. Gorelick, the microbiologist who ran the lab told Congress that the problem was infections that had taken place at the lab. According to Gorelick, "many of the agents with which we are working are exotic and/or newly discovered. There are usually no vaccines for preventing the disease nor drugs for treatment."

On at least one occasion. according to nonofficial base sources, volunteers at Fort Detrick staged a sit-down strike to protest incomplete information being offered to them about tests that they had been subjected to.

Between June 6 to 10, 1966 more than a million persons in New York City were exposed to bacillus subtilis variant niger when it was released in the subway system by the Army. The release was concentrated at Seventh Avenue and Eighth Avenue, at peak transit times. Light bulbs containing the bacteria were dropped onto ventilating grills and train roadbeds.

On March 13, 1968 an F4 Phantom jet flew over Dugway Proving Ground in Utah, dumping VX nerve gas from tanks slung beneath the craft. The entirety of the jet's cargo was not expended in the drop, and as it returned from its flight, approximately 20 pounds of nerve agents drifted on the wind, travelling thirty-five miles eastward of the plane's flight path. Ranchers in the area became sick and six thousand sheep grazing on private land died or had to be destroyed because of contamination.

The government, as is standard in such cases, denied that the accident had taken place, but the nerve agent VX was found in the animals when they were autopsied. The government still did not admit responsibility, but offered up to $1 million in damages to the owners of the sheep.

In 1971, the Cuban government claimed that the CIA had released African swine fever and dengue fever in Cuba, with 350,000 people becoming ill, and half a million pigs slaughtered to stop the epidemic. Although most of the government apologists who write histories of germ warfare say that this is an example of disinformation launched by the Cubans, it probably is not. In 1971 *Newsday* reported that an anonymous U.S. intelligence agent had delivered an unmarked canister to an area near the U.S. Navy base at Guantanamo. The outbreak of African swine fever in Cuba began six weeks later.

At the same time as the Cuban assault the U.S. provided the South Vietnamese government with riot control gases, including CS gas. CS was dropped by helicopter in fifty-five gallon drums in Vietnam offensives, with some 13.7 million pounds dropped in total during the Vietnam war. Nineteen million gallons of herbicides including Agents Orange, Blue, White, and Purple were also dumped on that country. After the war it was found that the herbicides did not cause the Viet Cong any food shortages, but it did severely deplete the ability of the peasants to raise food.

In November of 1969, President Richard Nixon announced that the U.S. would discontinue production of biological weapons, and destroy its stockpiles of those agents. A year later Nixon renounced the use of deadly toxins in warfare by the U.S. In truth, this was simply an exercise in expediency, since the relatively inexpensive production of biological weapons could be seen to particularly benefit nations lacking huge arsenals of conventional weapons.

According to Matthew Meselson, a professor of biochemistry at Harvard, and an expert on biological weapons, "The introduction of radically cheap weapons of mass destruction into the arsenals of the world would not act as much to strengthen the big powers as it would endow dozens of relatively weak countries with great destructive capacity."

In fact it had never been the intention of Nixon or the military establishment to discontinue biologicals testing. Now, however, the lion's share of research would be done through militarily-funded private enterprises under the umbrella of "defensive measures," much in the same way that CIA mind control operations were driven underground into "black" projects following their exposure at around the same time.

At the time of Nixon's announcement, Department of Defense spending on biowarfare research was increased from $21.9 to $23.2 million. Construction of facilities for biowarfare were also begun at Fort Detrick. In 1971 the U.S. Army Medical Research Institute of Infectious diseases was moved into the facility. This building became the principal area at

Fort Detrick for continued biowarfare development including genetic engineering of virulent microorganisms, all under the umbrella of defense.

The CIA also did not exactly adhere to the letter of Nixon's disavowal of bioweapons and toxins. The Company's stockpile of such agents were simply moved from Fort Detrick to the Huntington Research Center of the Becton-Dickinson Company in Baltimore Maryland.

In 1969 safety precautions were increased at Fort Detrick with the creation of isolated BL-4 labs or "hot suites."

Portions of Fort Detrick have become contaminated due to biological and chemical testing, including "The Tower," a seven-story building contaminated with anthrax. The building has not been entered in recent years except by monitors in protective gear who periodically confirm that the facility is anthrax-ridden and cannot be cleaned, much less occupied.

In 1989 another lab at Fort Detrick was quarantined, with 500 potentially ebola infected monkeys destroyed, a possible indication that the Army was experimenting with the ebola virus as a biowarfare weapon, certainly enough to give one pause to think, considering later ebola outbreaks among native populations.

By 1971 the Biological Weapons Convention was drafted, prohibiting the development and production of biological armaments and toxins. The Convention would eventually be agreed to by 118 nations although, again, the document may not have even slowed research and production in these areas. Genetic engineering of biological weapons, for instance, was not outlawed if this research was for "defensive" purposes.

In 1976 the Humane Society of Utah reported an incident where 50 wild horses had died after drinking from a spring located near the Dugway Proving Ground in Utah. Antigens caused by exposure to Venezuelan equine encephalomyelitis were also found in animals in areas around Dugway. And by 1986, as admitted by the Army, open air testing was again underway at Dugway.

Reports of the use of Soviet-produced "Yellow Rain" toxic agents on Laotian refugees in Thailand, made public in December 1979, provided one justification for increased congressional funding for the weapons of chemical warfare and the ending of its eighteen year moratorium on such production.

In 1984, Secretary of Defense Casper Weinberger stated that, "We continue to obtain new evidence that the Soviet Union has maintained its offensive biological warfare program and that it is exploring genetic engineering to expand their program's scope. Consequently, it is essential and urgent that we develop and field adequate biological and toxic protection."

Between the years 1980 and 1984 $50 million in funds for biological study were shifted from civilian organizations to the military.

In 1980 the Army advertised in *Science* magazine for proposals regarding "the introduction by recombinant DNA methods of the human nervous system gene of acetylcholinesterase from human neuroblastoma cells into a bacterium. The purpose of the research is to obtain a microorganism which synthesizes the human enzyme so that it can be isolated for biochemical, neurochemical, and pharmacological studies." Proposals were to be sent to Fort Detrick. Genetic research has been engaged in by the U.S. military since the 1950s, and according to scientists, has always run ten or more years ahead of discoveries in the private sector.

The Army had also sought and received permission from the National Institutes of Health advisory committee on recombinant DNA to conduct toxic research including experiments to clone toxins and the introduction of the pneumoccoccus toxin into E. coli bacteria. Also, guidelines were relaxed so that testing involving the release of genetically altered organisms into the environment was approved. By 1983 at least fourteen government-sponsored research programs into recombinant DNA were ongoing.

In August of 1984 the Army issued a report titled *Assessment of Chemical and Biological Sensor Technologies*. Although the greater portion of the report is devoted to the state of the art in biological detection devices, the report also suggests the resumption of field testing of biological warfare simulants, and does not suggest that these tests should be limited to non-populated areas.

In 1985 the Environmental Protection Agency approved two tests with genetically altered organisms, and after a court case delayed the tests, on April 24, 1987, the Advanced Genetic Sciences group sprayed bacteria over 2,500 strawberry plants in the Central Valley of California.

In July of 1984, Earl Davenport, a civilian worker at Dugway, participated in an outdoor test to determine if a laser could be used to detect chemical nerve agents. Davenport sprayed clouds of the "practically nontoxic" simulant DMMP into the beam of a laser. With a shift of the wind, Davenport was engulfed in a cloud of DMMP before he could don his protective mask. The following day he fell ill and checked into the University of Utah Hospital, where he was diagnosed with bronchial asthma that had probably been caused his exposure to the DMMP. Davenport had earlier in the year been documented as healthy by the Army, and he was using no medications at the time.

Three months after Davenport's exposure an assessment of the toxicity of DMMP on animals was done by scientists employed by the Army. The test concluded, "The lack of a no-effect dose... makes it impossible to establish a safety factor for use of the material. Based on these considerations recommend disapproval of DMMP for simulant testing."

This recommendation fell on deaf ears, since the Army did not discontinue usage of the substance as a simulant, including in open air testing.

Another report on the toxicity of DMMP was issued from Aberdeen Proving Ground, Maryland, in 1986. The report concluded,

"Considering the positive mutagenicity findings, the severe, dose related male reproductive hazard and the current finding of some carcinogenicity and renal toxicity in the male rat, the development of an acceptable PEL [permissible exposure limit] seems highly unlikely."

The report recommended the replacement of DMMP with an alternate agent although, again, the warning was not heeded. Instead the use of DMMP was merely "reduced significantly."

Earl Davenport has been plagued with health problems and, after a heart attack in 1988, his work with chemical and biological agents was terminated. In 1993 his condition had reached the point where he was advised that he could no longer work. When Davenport filed for workers' compensation, however, an examiner for the Department of Labor reported that the evidence "fails to establish that the claimed medical condition or disability is causally related to the injury," and that Davenport's disabilities had probably come about because he was a smoker.

In 1991 Dugway Proving Ground began doing outdoor testing using Yersinia pestis, the germ that causes bubonic plague. This disease organism, also known as the Black Death, has killed millions of persons over the past thousand years, and was responsible for wiping out three-quarters of the population of Europe and Asia in the Middle Ages. Still, the Army felt justified releasing these disease organisms into the air.

The Dugway Public Affairs Office announced that the strain of Yersinia, one that was deprived of iron, was a "relatively harmless" simulant and that it would be released outdoors. What Public Affairs didn't say was that studies conducted on mice showed that after they had been exposed to weakened strains of Yersinia, that they contracted the disease if they drank water with iron in it, thus reconstituting the disease organisms. According to Zell McGee, professor of medicine and pathology at the University of Utah Medical School, the same thing could happen with people.

By 1986, the U.S. military budget for chemical and biological weapons exceeded $1 billion.

A May, 1986 report to Congress listed the necessity for funding the BL-4 laboratory at Dugway Proving Grounds in Utah. An excerpt from the report provides a handy thumbnail sketch of research that was taking place at the facility at the time:

"— Viral pathogens could be constructed to maximize infectivity and pathogenicity. Infectious particles could be modified to increase or decrease their environmental stability, persistency and potency.

"— Naturally occurring protein toxins could be made in host organisms by modifying their DNA. Plant and/or fungal toxins could be mass produced.

"— Physiologically active peptides have significant potential to be developed for future biological warfare agents. They are active at very low concentrations. Their activity covers the full range of life processes, mental and physical.

"— Potent toxins, which until now were available only in minute quantities and only upon isolation from immense amounts of biological materials, can now be prepared in industrial quantities after a relatively short development period... as short as 9 months from concept to full-scale production. This process consists of identifying genes, encoding for the desired molecules, and transferring the sequence to a receptive microorganism which then becomes capable of producing the substance. The recombinant organisms may then be cultured and grown at any desired scale. They might be employed as agents themselves or used to produce toxins which can be extracted and concentrated.

"— Biotechnology could be used to alter the immunological character of agents for which vaccines have already been developed, thus circumventing protective properties of the vaccines.

"— It is possible to artificially produce the natural biological substances which exert potent regulatory effects on the body. These substances are normally present in the body in minute quantities and control mental states; mood and emotion; perception; organ function; growth and repair; temperature; and other body processes. These substances are not considered toxic and are indispensable for the normal functioning of the human body. But even slight imbalances can cause profound psychological effects, leading to incapacitation and death."

In 1997 the worldwide Chemical Weapons Convention (CWC), banning the use of chemical weapons, was endorsed by the world's superpowers, but in many ways this treaty is nothing more than a paper tiger. For instance, it does not even confront the threat of biological weapons. Currently, there are vague motions in the direction of a proposed Biological and Toxic Weapons Convention (BTWC), but there is little doubt that it will be years before a treaty of this nature will be ratified. Even then, what use do terrorist groups have for treaties or, for that matter, governments who feel it is in their interest to break such treaties?

# 6

## THE RED DEATH

L ike the United States, the Soviet Union has been engaged
in the development of chemical and biological weapons
since the 1940s. According to highly-placed Soviet dissidents
and defectors, since the 1950s it was recognized in the Soviet Union that biological and chemical weapons could be an
effective equivalent for nuclear weapons, only at far less of
a cost in terms of production.

There were other factors that militated for a heavy investment in CBW by the Reds. Soviet strategists knew that
these types of weapons were viewed by the U.S. with extreme repugnance, so that the possibility of a negotiated dis-
armament of the West was possible.

It was also considered that nuclear weapons might eventually be banned worldwide, at which time biowarfare capability would be the decisive factor in war. They also saw that
nuclear weapons might not be the ideal weapon to be used
against the People's Republic of China, due to that country's
enormous size and population; that biologicals in particular
would have advantages in a conflict with the PRC.

During the 1950s Soviet experimentation took place under the deepest cloak of secrecy, under program names such
as BUTTERFLY and SPRUCE, and where such programs
were explicitly referred to, they were called "special weapons" and "nuclear type 2" weapons in order to conceal their
actual nature.

By the 1960s chemical and biological weapons were one
of the highest military priorities throughout the Warsaw Pact.
Czechoslovakian programs were the spearhead of the Soviet
biowarfare capability, and in 1962 an institute was built there
entirely devoted to this type of research.

By 1964 Czechoslovak CBW weapons production, taking place in underground plants for the sake of security, was in full swing. One Czechoslovak weapons program supervised by the Soviets, in violation of the UN resolution forbidding such programs, was the delivery of CBW weapons from outer space.

According to the report of one of the highest ranking Soviet officers ever to defect to the West, the Czechoslovak political officer Major Jan Sejna, was privy to a conversation in 1963 between General Secretary Nikita Krushchev and Marshall Rodion Malinovsky. Malinovsky had just told the Soviet head, "Comrade Khrushchev, I believe socialism will be established and remain wherever Soviet tanks are present." Krushchev replied, "Between you and me there is a big difference. You would like to see Soviet tanks everywhere today. For me, tomorrow is sufficient. I don't want to burn Europe; I want German industry intact to build socialism."

For a long time, this in fact had been the policy of the Soviets, that the wide scale use of nuclear weapons would obliterate the prize: the possession of a Europe intact other than in its population. This of course is one of the "benefits" of CBW weaponry: it does not despoil the spoils of war.

In 1964 a twenty-year Soviet plan for the development of CBW weapons was completed, and these weapons were formally integrated into Warsaw Pact strategic plans. By 1967, weapons of these types were being tested in a Middle East exercise that took place at the same time as the Six-Day War.

At that time biological and chemical weapons were planned by the Russian to be primarily used for:
— (1) disabling regions and countries to prevent them from taking part in a war;
— (2) poisoning of locations where airborne troops would land;
— (3) to assassinate government elites
— (4) planned massive depopulation of the People's Republic of China
—(5) and for use in sabotage by Russia's elite *spetsnaz* and other Soviet special forces.

In the 1970s the Soviet Union had seen the wave of the future. They launched research programs into genetic engineering to create completely new biowarfare agents. Some of the developments that came out of this research were psychotoxins, neurotoxins, micro-proteins, and synthetic peptides, referred to as "the most malefic development in military toxicology." This is an area that still remains highly classified, and thus may hold many deadly surprises if deployment, that is, warfare, ever takes place.

At the same time that the Soviet biochemical warfare capability was growing by leaps and bounds, America abandoned its own research programs, shutting down its chemical warfare school, disbanding its Chemical Corps, and announcing that it would destroy its stock of weapons of that nature. In 1972 the U.S. signed the Biological and Toxin Weapons convention, and in 1975, signed the Geneva Protocol against the use of asphyxiating gas. The reason that America backed away from biowarfare capability was that American leadership had been deceived.

In the early '70s the FBI believed they had a highly-placed agent in the Soviet government, code-named "Fedora." Fedora relayed intelligence to the Americans that the Soviets, lacking much in the way of biochemical warfare capability and concerned about the far more advanced programs that the U.S. was presently engaged in, were considering upgrading their own capability. To discourage a CBW arms race, the U.S. dismantled its own stockpiles and most of its research. It is now understood that Fedora was a double agent in the employ of the KGB, and that the plan from the beginning had been to encourage the Americans to discontinue their research. The Soviets, of course, continued with their own research and stockpiling of the deadly agents.

Although there were many signs that the U.S. had been the victim of a ruse, it was not until 1979 that the government realized it. That was when an explosion at a Soviet biowarfare plant in Sverdlovsk, Cantonment 19, released a cloud of pulmonary anthrax bacilli or anthrax spores over the neighboring territory, killing between two hundred and a thousand people.

At about the same time, reports coming from Southeast Asia were noted by U.S. officials. Those reports were of a "Yellow Rain" that had been falling on and killing hill tribes and other anti-Soviet combatants in Vietnam, Laos, and Kampuchea. The Yellow Rain operations were later described by a Lao People's Liberation Army officer, who indicated that they were code-named "extinction destruction operations." According to the defected officer, the operations were overseen by Vietnamese officers.

After the invasion of Afghanistan by the Soviets in December 1979, reports were received of the same deadly Yellow Rain being used against Afghan refugees and medical personnel helping with the evacuation. The Yellow Rain is reported to have made the skin of the infected so soft that fingers could be pushed through it.

When the Yellow Rain was analyzed, mycotoxins were detected. A Soviet soldier also testified to chemicals that had been used in the Yellow Rain. He said that there were at least three: picric acid, asphyxiating gases, and a chemical described only as "100 percent lethal." Finally, the U.S. military establishment realized that they had been taken in by the Soviet's strategic deception.

The first disclosure of new Soviet biochemical warfare capabilities to the American public came in 1983, when newspaper columnist Jack Anderson wrote about a top secret CIA assessment of the Soviet use of gene splicing to produce "super-viruses more deadly than any known to man today."

Another revelation that came out at the same time was from a Soviet immigrant who said that scientists in Russia were attempting to splice genes that produced toxins into the DNA of the common flu bug.

In response to information about the new Soviet warfare capability, Congress voted to increase funds for research into genetic engineering. By 1988 there were at least 99 U.S. military programs researching genetic engineering for the purpose of warfare.

One breakthrough in Soviet biochemical warfare was noted by the Presidential Chemical Warfare Review Commission in 1985. It was reported that the Soviets had accomplished their long term goal of finding warfare agents that would penetrate Western gas masks and protective clothing. Michael Waller, a senior fellow of the American Foreign Policy Council, while travelling in Russia in 1993 met one Vladimir Petrenko. Petrenko claimed that he had volunteered for Soviet experimentation with a Soviet superpoison named Novichok, which allegedly affected human genes. Petrenko's claims were later backed up by Val Mirzaynov, a Russian scientist who claimed to have participated in the creation of Novichok.

Mirzayanov also spoke about another poisonous agent, Substance A-230, whose potency supposedly surpasses any other military toxin by a factor of five to eight times. According to Mirzaynov, tests of A-230 were conducted at a facility near Nukus, Uzbekistan in 1989.

Mirzayanov also spoke of other chemical weapons including a binary weapon (composed of two chemicals that become lethal when combined) called Substance 33, and Substance A-232, reportedly another weapon of the Novichok class.

On April 9, 1989, Soviet troops from the Ministries of Defense and the Interior used chemical weapons, what they claimed was tear gas, on 8,000 to 10,000 protestors in Tbilisi, Soviet Georgia. Twenty people died from the "tear gas" and four more from injuries, with many hundreds more hospitalized at the time. Literally thousands more victims, including hundreds of school children who were accidentally caught in the line of dispersion of the gas, continued to apply to hospitals in the months to come.

An International Committee of the Red Cross investigative team led by Dr. Andrei Sakharov called for additional investigation of the incident by the Physicians for Human Rights. The PHR confirmed that tear gas, specifically CN and CS gas, had been employed on the demonstrators, but they also determined that a third agent, chloropicrin, was used. Chloropicrin is a much more toxic chemical that causes skin and respiratory blisters, prevents breathing, and causes pulmonary edema.

In 1998 information received from a Russian defector further updated the world on Soviet biological warfare preparations. Ken Alibek, formerly Kanatjan Alibekov, the former deputy director of a Soviet biological weapons program, stated that biological weapons were continuing to be developed in Russia. Alibek also said that the Soviet Union had "hundreds of tons" of anthrax, smallpox, and plague viruses, and that missiles carrying biowarfare bacteria had been aimed at the U.S. in 1992, the year of his defection. Whether the missiles were still aimed at America, Alibek did not know.

According to Alibek, the biowarfare weapon that had been of most interest to the Soviets was smallpox. This was convenient, in that international health officials had in 1979 stated that the world was free of smallpox, thus ending the production of vaccines for the virus, and assuring deadly results if the germ was dispersed during warfare.

In March, 1994 the *London Sunday Times* reported the Russian creation of what they termed "superplague powder," an agent that was otherwise unspecified, but was claimed to have no known antidote.

The Soviet Union has also been implicated in the training of terrorists in the use and production of CBW agents. As of 1980, the USSR was reported to have been training a minimum of 1,200 terrorists in Moscow, and many of these individuals are known to have migrated to the U.S., where it is not entirely improbable that some may be functioning as deep cover agents for sneak attack. With the vast influx of Soviets as well as other national groups to the United States in recent years, this country is wide open for sabotage.

One major headache for the U.S. is the concern that Russian chemical and biowarfare experts, some of whom have become somewhat desperate, having gone without pay recently, are willing to export their deadly expertise to other countries.

Another problem that experts in biowarfare have become aware of is the lack of security at Russian military installations since the supposed downfall of the Soviet bloc. One such location is the Vector base in Siberia. According to World Health Organization scientist D.A. Henderson, "Vector was once protected by well-armed guards and barbed wire fences, but the barbed wire is gone now and the guards, who haven't been paid in months, can be persuaded with a little vodka."

One biowarfare agent that is stored at Vector is smallpox. Henderson said, "First, you should be reminded that the last smallpox vaccination in this country [America] was administered in 1972. The only people vaccinated over the next eight years were workers in hospitals or laboratories, but by and large few people have been vaccinated since 1972 and I would suspect only ten to fifteen percent of the U.S. population have antibodies to the disease."

The scientist also commented about anthrax, suggesting that it was a particularly appropriate weapon for use by terrorists: "Their particular interest is because anthrax is so easily acquired and so easily mass-produced. There are nations and dissident groups that have both access to the biological agents and people intelligent enough to know the means of deploying them. Even small groups can wreak considerable havoc, and they are prepared to do so."

# 7

## YELLOW RAIN
## AND OTHER ATROCITIES

A fter the fall of Saigon, and between June 1976 and May 1979, the Vietnamese set about on a process of genocide of the Hmong tribespeople of Laos. Fifteen to twenty thousand Hmong were murdered with "Yellow Rain" nerve gas dropped from airplanes. The nerve gas—of at least two and possibly three types—were provided by the Soviets.

### CUBA

Oscar Alcalde Ledon, a Cuban escaping from the island and the former director of the Cuban Academy of Science, in 1963 said that Cuba was preparing a germ warfare attack on the United States. This is hardly surprising, since the U.S. has credibly been linked to biowarfare attacks on that country. The specific weapon was reportedly being prepared in a secret lab at Soroa, in the Pinar Del Rio province. Alcalde quoted Cuban officials as saying that "it is now very easy for the Cuban government to introduce foot and mouth disease into the United States."

At least two underground biological-chemical warfare facilities exist in Cuba. One is at Kimonor, in the Matanzas province. This facility was built by the Soviets in 1981 and in the past has been supplied with Soviet instructors. Cuban nationals are not allowed entry into this facility. This plant is reported to have produced Yellow Rain and other biochemical agents, with the product being shipped to counties including the Soviet Union, Afghanistan, Poland, and East Germany.

Another biochemical facility is at Jardin de Orquilles, near the town of Soroa. Biological warfare agents and toxins have been produced here, with the toxins described as being appropriate for poisoning the water supplies of cities. Instructors at the Cuban Revolutionary Army chemical warfare school have stated that toxins placed in the Mississippi River could poison one third of the United States.

Members of the PLO and SWAPO have also been trained in chemical warfare techniques in Cuba.

### EGYPT

This country first acquired chemical and biological weapons in the early 1960s from the Soviets. In 1963 through 1967 there were reports of Egypt using Soviet-supplied chemical agents against the opposition in Yemen. Mustard gas, phosgene, and perhaps other agents were dropped on civilian targets, killing and injuring thousands. Despite many reports of chemical weapons attacks by the Egyptians, no protests were heard in the U.N. or in the Establishment-controlled media in America.

When Israelis searched Egyptian bunkers during the Six Day War, large quantities of stored nerve gas that had been provided by the Soviets were found.

### LIBYA

Libya is said to be currently producing biological warfare agents in large quantities. Libyan operatives were arrested in the late 1980s attempting to buy sterile environment equipment in the U.S. that could have been used in the production of biowarfare agents. Libya is also reported to have used chemical weapons in a war against Chad in 1987.

According to a number of reports, France provided Libya with a ton of the deadly nerve agent Tabun for their stockpiles.

### NORTH KOREA

In September of 1994 the South Korean government issued claims that North Korea was engaged in testing chemical weapons on political prisoners. According to the South Koreans, their enemy possessed one thousand tons of chemical warfare agents. They also claimed that the North Koreans were working to extend the range of their missiles, doubling their range to 1,250 miles, and placing Japan within range. In a way this is old news, since reliable military intelligence within recent months has shown that the North Koreans, within approximately two years, will have missiles capable of hitting all 50 United States.

# 8

## IRAQI STORM CLOUDS

In 1967 Iraq petitioned the Soviet Union for nuclear weapons to counter the perceived threat of Israeli nuclear capability. The Soviets chose not to provide nuclear weapons, but instead, in the fall of 1967, decided to provide CBW agents to their ally instead.

Iraq was also reaching out to Western countries for the components to build chemical and biological weapons. By the late 1970s Iraq had obtained equipment and chemicals necessary for the creation of biowarfare weapons from a number of countries including Belgium, Italy, the Netherlands, Switzerland and, particularly, West Germany.

Among the allegations of Western companies that supplied Iraq: Technical help is said to have been obtained from the Fritz Werner Company; piping, vessels, and centrifuges from Quast GmbH; chemicals and pumps from Water Engineering Trading GmbH; and the Karl Kolb Company built a state of the art "pesticide" plant that would be used for constructing weapons.

An article in the *Houston Chronicle*, referred to statements made by Senator Donald W. Riegle Jr. of Michigan,

"During the 1980s, the U.S. government approved shipments of biological agents to Iraq... The viruses and bacteria, commonly used to develop biological weapons, were shipped directly to Iraqi government agencies by American Type Culture Collection, a nonprofit group in Rockville, MD, that collects and distributes biological specimens worldwide. Virtually all the shipments, Riegle said, were approved by the Reagan administration's Commerce Department between 1985 and 1989 despite long-standing suspicions that Iraq had been involved in biological warfare."

Incredibly, shipments of deadly viruses were also sent by the Centers for Disease Control via Express Mail to Iraq, Cuba, China, and the Soviet Union, and Dr. Garth Nicholson has said that microbiologists from Iraq working on germ warfare were also trained in the U.S., some of them by the Department of Defense.

Not only did the U.S. supply germ warfare agents to Iraq, they also provided the wherewithal to buy them. Sarah McLendon, writing in *Media Bypass* magazine, reported that a $5 billion dollar loan to Iraq from the BNL Italian Bank of Rome was guaranteed by the U.S., using taxpayers' money, through the Department of Agriculture's Commodity Credit Corp. This loan was transformed into Letters of Credit that were used to buy weapons, including biological warfare agents and SCUD missiles from the U.S. When Iraq defaulted on the loan, the U.S. covered for them and wrote off the debt!

After the Israeli destruction of the Osirak reactor in Iraq in 1981, the possibility of an Iraqi nuclear capability was severely set back, and so Saddam Hussein redoubled his efforts in the area of biochemical warfare. A chemical weapons production factory was built near Baghdad, dubbed the SEPP (State Establishment for the Production of Pesticides). Equipment and chemical components for weaponry were provided by "the whole world," according to an engineer from the German Hammer Company who worked at SEPP.

Among the companies that lined up to improve Saddam's biochemical warfare capacity were ones located in Germany, France, Great Britain, Australia, Poland, India, and the United States, this last with the approval of the U.S. government.

By 1982 SEPP was producing mustard gas, and sarin and tabun nerve agents, definitely a case of overkill when used as pesticides for food production. These are the same weapons agents that evidence suggests were used against American soldiers during the Gulf War.

Another firm that provided biologicals to Iraq, according to Dr. Garth Nicolson, was Tanox Biosystems. Tanox is said to be partly owned by James Baker III, the former Secretary of State under George Bush. Baker is reported to have been involved in the sale of large quantities of biological components to Iraq prior to the Gulf War.

Tanox reportedly was involved in experimenting with Mycoplasma fermentans (incognitus). Experimentation using this agent is alleged to have been done on inmates of death row at the Huntsville, Texas State Prison. According to Nicolson, after the testing was done on inmates, the disease spread to members of the general prison population, to guards, and to the families of guards. At this time there are reported to be 350 persons in the Huntsville, Texas area infected with this bacterial agent.

Also documented as assisting in the Iraqi unconventional weapons program include Hewlett Packard, Alcolac International, and the Al Haddad Trading Company. In addition, at least *2.8 billion* in grants from the U.S. was used to finance Iraq's military expansion. As a slap on the wrist, the export of chemicals that could be used to make chemical weapons was banned by the United States and several other nations, but even the ban on the export of chemicals was bypassed. The simple fact was that the reason for the light treatment of Iraq was that the U.S. wanted Saddam Hussein to remain as a strong force in the region, in part to offset the power of Iran.

Iraq is reported to have first begun the use of chemical warfare during the Iran-Iraq War in 1980, with mustard gas being the major chemical used. By 1984 an unexploded Iraqi bomb containing the nerve agent tabun was discovered by a U.N. inspection team. Other nerve agents were used in the February 1986 defense of the Fao peninsula, in which casualties were reported as being as high as 5,000 in one day.

Even when presented with evidence that the Iraqis were using chemical warfare, the 207 documented firms in 21 countries that were supplying the Iraqis with equipment, technical expertise, and precursors for chemical weaponry, did not curtail their trade in those commodities. Such is the power of the dollar.

Iraq was not officially censured for its use of nerve agents and other chemical weapons, possibly because the chemicals and equipment that had been used to construct the chemical weapons had been imported from Western countries, and this would have led to investigations that would have been uncomfortable for those in positions of power.

After the Iran-Iraq war had ended, in March, 1988, a Kurdish rebellion in Iraq was defeated by the use of mustard and nerve gas. Five thousand deaths are reported as having taken place in the Iraqi town of Halabja.

In 1988 the first public concerns were voiced that Iraq was delving into the creation of biological weapons: specifically typhoid, cholera, and anthrax. Iraq's biological weapons production was taking place at Salman Pak, about 40 miles from Baghdad.

In 1990 it was revealed that the U.S. Centers for Disease Control and Prevention (CDC) had shipped more than 80 deadly biological materials including botulinium toxoid and the West Nile fever virus to Iraq in the 1980s. Also, during the same period, the American Type Culture Collection (ATCC) shipped virulent bacteria (including those that cause tetanus, anthrax, and botulism) as well as toxins to Iraq's Atomic Energy Commission, Ministry of Trade, Ministry of Higher Education, and the State Company for Drug Industries.

Also included in American government-sanctioned sales to Iraq were the following biowarfare agents: Bacillus anthracis, Clostridium botulinum, histoplasma capsulatum, Brucella melitensis, and Clostridium perfringens, and E-coli.

According to the United Nations Special Commission on Munitions (UNSCOM), Iraq has engaged in a particularly sinister line of research: the use of CBW warfare not to kill but to slowly disable. The commission reports that beginning in 1988 Iraq delved deeply into the use of fungal toxins, particularly aflatoxin (produced by Asperfillus flavus, a wheat and peanut crop contaminant) for use in war. Testing at the Al Salman facility in Iraq indicated that high concentrations of aflatoxin brought about a swift death, but that low concentrations of the toxin caused the victim to develop liver cancer, as well as to experience bizarre symptoms that did not fit into any other known disease profile. Low dosages of afla-toxin caused flu-like symptoms that lasted for only a short while, followed by "aggressively metastasizing neoplasms" some years later. This, in itself, is a biowarfare strategy that can be used to disable entire populations, even over a period of decades. Disease epidemics that are gradually adminis-tered will be seen as naturally occurring, and not as an attack by a hostile foreign power.

By 1990, Iraq had produced an estimated 572 gallons of aflatoxin. More than 410 gallons is said to have been loaded into munitions such as R400 aerial bombs and SCUD-B ex-tended range missiles, some of which would be used against American troops.

# 9

## CONFLAGRATION

Iraq invaded Kuwait on August 2, 1990. Earlier, it is alleged, America's ambassador to Iraq practically gave the green light to Saddam for a Kuwaiti invasion, but as soon as it had happened America changed her tune in an apparent act of betrayal. The whole thing may have been a setup to neutralize Saddam, whose potential control of twenty percent of the world's oil supplies greatly concerned and still concerns the U.S.

After Saddam Hussein rejected demands from the U.S. to withdraw from the country, American President George Bush organized a war coalition of 37 countries to forcibly remove Iraqi forces from Kuwait. Bush, in a ploy similar to that recently performed by President Clinton on the leader of Yugoslavia, characterized Saddam as a modern day Hitler. Amusingly, that characterization may have only improved Saddam's image at home. According to journalist Elaine Sciolino, the Iraqis had backed Hitler during World War II and, "As Iraqis saw it, Hitler's only fault was that he lost the war."

The New World Order's war on Iraq began on January 17, 1991, and lasted 43 days. George Bush was nervous about Iraq's stockpiles of chemical and biological weapons, and this was perhaps exemplified by a Secret Service agent who accompanied Bush on the day the war began. The agent carried a gas mask in a green military bag for the president's protection. Bush was in Washington, D.C. at the time.

According to a report of the Department of Defense to Congress in 1992,

"By the time of the invasion of Kuwait, Iraq had developed biological weapons. Its aggressive biological warfare program was the most advanced in the Arab world. [The] program probably began in the late 1970s and concentrated

on the development of two agents — botulinum toxin and anthrax bacteria... Large scale production of these agents began in 1989 at four facilities near Bagdad. Delivery means
for biological agents ranged from simple aerial bombs and
artillery rockets to surface to surface missiles."

The U.S and its Allies were virtually unprepared against
CBW agents, despite the fact that the U.S. military was well
aware of Iraq's use of nerve and mustard gas against Iran in
the 1980s. Troops leaving for the Gulf War received inoculations against anthrax and botulinum toxin. Some of them were
also provided with gas masks and protective clothing, although
this protective gear was primarily outdated equipment from
the early 1960s, and was often not worn in dangerous areas,
according to the reports of many servicemen.

Although the standard texts about the Gulf War state that
Iraq did not deploy chemical or biological weapons against
the U.S. and its allies, this does not seem to be the case.

# 10

## AFTERMATH

According to a report of H. Lindsey Arison III, Ph.D., a civilian advisor to the Under Secretary of the U.S. Air Force,
"Chemical warfare munitions and agents which either survived the allied bombings or were inventoried and returned to the Muthanna (Iraq) facility for destruction included:
"— 13,000 155-mm artillery shells loaded with mustard gas (H).
"— 6,200 rockets loaded with nerve agent.
"— 800 nerve agent aerial bombs.
"— 28 SCUD warheads loaded with nerve agent Sarin (GB).
"— 75 tons of nerve agent Sarin (GB).
"— 60-70 tons of nerve agent Tabun (GA), and
"— 250 tons of mustard gas and stocks of thiodiglycol, a precursor for mustard gas."
Based on information in U.N. documents, despite efforts to stop biological and chemical warfare research in Iraq, their programs of research and production in these areas continues on a covert basis. As of February, 1998, the U.N. Special Commission (UNSCOM) had found and destroyed 127,000 gallons of chemicals that could be used in the production of chemical weapons. But there are, at the minimum, six hundred tons of precursor chemicals that are still unlocated that could be used to produce two hundred tons of VX nerve gas, a quantity sufficient to kill every person on this planet.
Iraq also maintains that it destroyed four tons of VX that had been earlier produced, but there is no way of confirming this. There are four thousand tons of precursor chemicals that could be used to produce hundreds of tons of chemical

weapons other than VX that are not accounted for. There are seventeen tons of growth media for anthrax that are unaccounted for.

As far as delivery systems, some believe that Iraq still has approximately two dozen missiles and mobile launchers hidden away. This, to me, is not the most terrifying of possibilities, since there are other far less expensive and undetectable means of employing CBW weapons.

Iraqi officials, although admitting to having constructed biowarfare weapons, maintain that they were all destroyed in 1991. By November of 1997, so much evidence had been amassed proving the existence of a biowarfare arsenal, including the shipping of tons of biological growth medium from Western companies after the Gulf War, that Saddam's only recourse was to throw U.N. inspectors out of the country.

Another aspect of Iraq's research into biowarfare was revealed in a *CBS Evening News* broadcast and a subsequent *Times Wire Service* article from 1998. According to the article,

"A U.S. intelligence official confirmed Wednesday that Iraq is attempting to develop an unmanned aircraft that could be used to deliver biological weapons on targets as far away as Israel...

"The U.S. official, who spoke on condition of anonymity, said Iraq is trying to convert an L-29 trainer jet into an unmanned delivery system for the biological agent anthrax. The jet would have a range of about 500 miles, long enough to reach targets in Israel as well as most of the U.S. forces in the Persian Gulf.

"But one version of the aircraft recently crashed in a test flight, according to the televised report, and Iraq has not yet developed a container to carry the biological agent. Iraq is required by United Nations resolutions to destroy its long-range missiles, but there is no ban against an unmanned aircraft."

Shortly after the Gulf War, Iraq is said to have used mustard gas on mobs rebelling against the rule of Saddam Hussein. After the Gulf War Iraq admitted to the United Nations that it had nearly 10,000 nerve gas warheads, 1,000 tons of mustard and nerve gas, 1,500 chemical bombs, and thirty missiles with chemical warheads. U.N. inspectors found that this was a gross underestimate of Iraq's stockpiles, much of which was otherwise unaccounted for.

In March of 1998, whether in a false alarm or not, the British newspaper *The Sun* reported that Saddam Hussein had sent Iraqi agents to Britain to disperse anthrax.

# 11

## GULF WAR SYNDROME

Although the facts are carefully hidden and denied by government and the mainstream media, a plague has struck 27 of the 28 countries that were involved in the Gulf War. Dr. Garth Nicholson, the David Bruton Jr. Chair in Cancer Research, and Professor and Chairman of the Department of Tumor Biology, the University of Texas (along with a host of other credentials) estimates that as many as 200,000 of the troops that were sent to Desert Storm are now infected with what is termed Gulf War Illness, and that 15,000 of those involved in the conflict have already died. Also, it is estimated that approximately half, or 51,000 of the 100,000 reservists and members of the National Guard who served in the Gulf War are ill with GWI. In excess of 160,000 Gulf War veterans have reported their illness to the Gulf War Registry.

Pinpointed in terms of the highest percentage of victims of GWI among American forces, are the 101st Airborne, the 82nd Airborne, the 3rd and 5th Special Forces, and the Big Red One out of Fort Riley, Kansas.

Among the symptoms of this Gulf War plague that can appear from six months to seven years later, are chronic fatigue, vomiting and diarrhea, severe joint pains, headaches, loss of memory, insomnia, rashes, swollen lymph nodes, tumors including those of the brain stem, problems of the nervous system, bizarre changes in the personality, and the wasting away of the body. Some victims of GWI are bleeding from every orifice in their body, much as victims of the ebola virus do. In many ways, the symptoms of GWI have been compared to AIDS. It is estimated that as many as 50% of sufferers commit suicide.

Many experts believe that the Gulf War Illness is communicable, with an accurate estimate of the number of family members and associates infected impossible to determine.
Thousands of infants born to Gulf War veterans, up to 50% of
them, are born dead, deformed, or with blood disorders.

According to a study done by U.S. Senator Don Riegle,
78% of the wives of Desert Storm veterans are sick, 25% of
their children born prior to the war are sick, and 65% of their
children born after the war are also sick.

But in spite of all the evidence and presumably out of
concern for having to compensate victims of GWI, the government is hiding what is going on. In August of 1992 three
health referral centers were set up by the Department of
Veterans' Affairs in Washington, D.C., Houston, and Los
Angeles. Their purpose was to evaluate a wide range of unusual symptoms of illness that veterans of the Gulf War were
reporting. The government issued reports that these symptoms were psychosomatic, or were caused by inhaling the
smoke from burning wells. Later it was said that the illness
came from leishmaniasis, a parasite that is transmitted by
sandfly bites. Within the next few years, a parade of excuses
for what had come to be known as Gulf War Syndrome were
trotted out by the military, including exposure to fuel, pesticides, and chemical sensitivity. Government experts were
willing to pinpoint almost any cause for the diseases which
were occurring, in fact, except for the obvious one: exposure
to chemical and biological agents.

Congressional hearings were held in 1993, and a number
of Gulf War vets told of illness since the war. One example
was Colonel Herbert J. Smith, who had been in fine health
prior to his participation in the war, but afterward became
sick with swollen glands, coughing, and aching in his joints.
Cole's sickness had gotten so bad that he was experiencing
memory loss and was unable to walk in a straight line. Smith
was told by an army neurologist that his problems were related to old age — Smith was 50 in 1991, the time of the
diagnosis.

Smith had a different opinion. He had seen dead animals covered with dead flies in the war zone, and had come to believe that he had been exposed to chemicals or biological weaponry.

There are many other credible reports of Iraqi chemical/biological attack upon servicemen fighting in the Gulf War. Another example is that of Willie Hicks, who served with the 644th Ordinance Company as a non-commissioned officer. In testimony before the Senate Committee on Armed Services' Subcommittee for Force Structure and Personnel, Hicks said that on January 17, 1991 he heard a loud explosion that was followed by alarms going off in the outpost he was in. As he ran for cover, Hicks reports that he felt his face burning and that one member of his unit also seeking cover "just dropped."

Within two to three days Hicks was sick, and exhibited blood in his urine. When he and other members of his unit attempted to talk to their superiors about what had taken place, they were ordered to keep quiet about the matter.

According to a staff report for U.S. Senator Donald W. Riegle, Jr., in September of 1993, 85 of the unit's 110 soldiers now suffer from medical problems. Hicks has also reported on one member of the unit who was formerly in good health, and then suddenly died.

Hicks himself is now experiencing a variety of problems including severe memory loss, and going unconscious, which has caused him to quit his job. According to the Veterans Administration, he is suffering from traumatic stress disorder.

Another account of probable CBW warfare during the Gulf War is that of Petty Officer Sterling Symms, who at the time was assigned to the Naval Reserve Construction Battalion 24, near the Kuwaiti border. On January 20, 1991, according to Symms, there was an explosion overhead and alarms sounded in the camp. As Symms ran toward a protective bunker he noticed the sharp smell of ammonia in the air, and felt his eyes and skin burning. Symms and the rest of his unit put on chemical protective gear, not taking it off for two hours, until an "all clear" signal was given.

Later, members of the unit were told that what they had heard had merely been a sonic boom. Symms finds this explanation rather implausible, seeing as how there was a visible fireball from the explosion. Members of the unit were also ordered not to discuss what happened.

Since the occurrence, Symms has experienced fatigue, a chronic rash, and open sores, among other symptoms. According to Symms, other members of the unit as well as some of their wives have also been treated for the same problems.

The smoking gun in terms of Gulf War Illness is the identification by Dr. Garth L. Nicholson and his wife, Dr. Nancy L. Nicholson, of the specific biological agent involved in GWI. After testing thousands of the blood samples of veterans, the Nicholsons found about half the samples infected with Mycoplasma fermentans (incognitus), a germ agent that includes most of the HIV envelope gene, but which is far more communicable than AIDS. GWI can be spread by sex, through perspiration, by simple contact, or by the aerial borne germs of coughing or sneezing.

According to the Nicholsons, in a paper titled "Chronic Fatigue Illness and Desert Storm—Were Biological Weapons Used Against Our Forces in the Gulf War?,"

"Not every Gulf War veteran had the same type of mycoplasma DNA sequences that came from mycoplasmas bound to or inside their white blood cells. Of particular importance, however, was our detection of highly unusual retroviral DNA sequences in the same samples by the same technique. These highly unusual DNA sequences included a portion of the HIV-1 (the AIDS-causing virus) genetic code, the HIV-1 envelope gene, but not the entire HIV-1 viral genomes.

"The type of mycoplasma we identified was highly unusual and it almost certainly could not occur naturally. It has one gene from the HIV-1 virus—but only one gene. This meant

it was almost certainly an artificially modified microbe—
altered purposely by scientists to make them more pathogenic and more difficult to detect.

"Thus these soldiers were not infected with the HIV-1
virus, because the virus cannot replicate with only the HIV-1
envelope gene that we detected... Such findings suggest that
the mycoplasmas that we have found in Gulf War veterans
are not naturally occurring organisms, or to be more specific, they were probably genetically modified or 'engineered'
to be more invasive and pathogenic, or quite simply, more
potent biological weapons."

Supporting the idea that mycoplasmas were used for biological warfare is the information that these agents have been
manufactured for at least fifteen years by Iraq and other countries including the U.S., China, Russia, Israel, and Libya.

There are, apparently, a number of causes of Gulf War
Illness. The largest percentage of cases of GWI among Gulf
War soldiers and others were probably caused by exposure
to chemical and biological weapons agents delivered by Iraqi
missile, artillery, and other attacks, and by contamination
from the bombing of Iraqi production and storage facilities
for chemicals and biologicals.

Another cause of GWI appears to have been untested
drugs and vaccines that were forcibly administered to the
troops of 27 of the 28 countries that participated in the Gulf
War. These drugs and vaccines included previously untested
pyridostigmine bromine pills (ostensibly as protection against
nerve agents), botulinum, anthrax, and other experimental
vaccines. The only country whose troops were not so dosed
was France. Another factor contributing to the lack of GWI
in French troops is that they were dosed with doxycycline
prior to the war, and after suspected exposure to biological
agents.

# 1 2

## AIDS as a Biowarfare Weapon

In *Los Angeles Times* of May 20, 1996 appeared an article titled "Report Warns of Global Health Crisis," subtitled "Infectious Diseases: Despite Medical Advances, Millions Are Dying." The article reported that,

"Declaring a 'global crisis' and warning that 'no country is safe from infectious diseases,' the World Health Organization says in a new report that diseases such as AIDS, ebola, hanta, mad cow, tuberculosis, etc. killed more than 17 million people worldwide last year, including 9 million children.

"Taken together, bacterial, viral and parasitic diseases remain the world's leading cause of premature death, accounting for one out of every three deaths, the report says. For instance, the No. 1 infectious diseases, tuberculosis, took 3.1 million lives last year, up 400,000 from WHO figures for 1993.

"The report also suggests with uncommon starkness that in today's global community, populations mix with unprecedented ease, and disease organisms have the potential to spread among countries at jet speed. Among the reasons that many infectious diseases are spreading so rapidly, the WHO report says, are growing antibiotic resistance and heavy international air travel."

The above information is true, but it is incomplete. The whole truth is far more ugly and far more shocking, for many of the deadly plagues that are now rearing their heads are man-made.

Vying with a number of other ugly candidates for the greatest conspiracy cover-up of the century is the history of AIDS. Although estimates vary widely, according to the International AIDS Center at Harvard, as many as 110 million people will be infected with AIDS by the time of the publication of this book. The CIA has estimated that 75% of the population of Africa living south of the Sahara Desert is infected with AIDS at this time. The greatest horror of it is that, since the appearance of AIDS in 1977 in Africa, many competent researchers have suggested that the virus was manmade.

The closest thing to an official explanation for AIDS is the African Green Monkey theory, which concludes that the disease was first transmitted to a human in Africa through a monkey bite, through eating monkey flesh, or through sexual contact with the animals. Many experts dispute that this could have been the origin of the virus. Dr. Seymour Kalter, one of the world's leading experts in monkey virology, at a Frederick Cancer Research Center symposium, has stated that the only danger to humans from simian monkey viruses is when that virus has contaminated a vaccine, and is then injected.

Another prominent dissenting voice is that of Dr. Robert Strecker. In an interview, Dr. Strecker explains the situation:

"What convinced us was the fact that this new agent had suddenly appeared out of nowhere. That the virus had characteristics of animal viruses more so than human viruses, and that the genetic structure of the AIDS virus actually looked like the viruses that appeared in animals that would not normally adapt themselves in humans...

"That could have occurred spontaneously, but not by the process that scientists have normally talked about. For instance, not by the virus running in primates because if you look at the genetic structure of the AIDS virus, what you find is that the codon choices [that designates the production of specific amino acids by the infected cell] included in the AIDS virus are not existent in primate genes.

"Therefore, to assume that they simply mutated in order to adapt themselves into primates in the case of AIDS is vanishingly small although still possible.

"What happened is that the virus either mutated in cattle and sheep, and then was artificially adapted to humans by growing in human tissue cultures, which they [virologists] do and in which they are easily manipulated in that manner — or the virus was actually constructed in a laboratory by gene manipulation, which was available to scientists in the early '70s although many of the techniques were not talked about until the mid '70s, because the biowarfare laboratories throughout the world have always been about five to ten years ahead of other laboratories.

"In addition, a clearer reason is, if you look at the appearance of the 'human retroviruses,' the fact is that there were a host of these things that appeared all at the same time. So, you have to explain not only the appearance of HIB-I, but also HIV-II, HTLV-I, HTLV-II, HTLV-IV, HTLV-V, HTLV-VI, ad nauseam.

"And so, to say that these things all spontaneously mutated at the same time in nature, and in the same direction, to infect human beings spontaneously and spread disease in worldwide epidemic proportions, in my opinion, is absurd compared to the known fact that scientists were working with exact progenitors of these viruses in their laboratories, which we can document."

Speculation that AIDS had begun as a specifically targeted bio-weapon surfaced in the alternative and gay press shortly after the onset of the disease, with the gay newspaper, the *New York Native* printing an anonymous letter from a person who claimed to have worked at Fort Detrick. The source maintained that AIDS had been developed and released as part of an offensive against gay men called "Operation Firm Hand."

The first widely-disseminated claim that AIDS had been developed as a biowarfare weapon came in 1984, when the New Delhi *Patriot* released details about research by the U.S. Army into "natural and artificial influences on the human immune system." The contention of the article was that scientists from the Army research laboratory at Fort Detrick, Maryland had travelled to Africa in search of new, virulent viruses, and that the samples and information gathered allowed the isolation of the AIDS virus. An anonymous American anthropologist was quoted to support the scenario, as well as quotes confirming the thesis culled from the Army's magazine *Army Research Development and Acquisition.*

In 1986 two French scientists working in East Germany, Jakob and Lilli Segal, released a 52-page pamphlet titled "AIDS: USA Home-Made Evil," that, like the article in the Indian newspaper, claimed that the virus had been manufactured at Fort Detrick. The Segals claimed that AIDS was a designer virus, a hybrid of visan virus in sheep, and HTLV-1, a white blood cell cancer.

Many factors support the theory of AIDS as biowarfare. The vectors of the disease are particularly damning to the 'accidental' theory, suggesting a planned biowarfare or depopulation approach: The virus targets homosexuals, intravenous drug users, and Africans.

One particularly damning corroboration of the idea that AIDS was intentionally foisted upon the world is in the records of a meeting of the House Subcommittee on Military Appropriations for June 9, 1969. At that meeting Dr. Donald MacArthur, Deputy Director for the Department of Defense Research and Technology, sought funding for a pet project. MacArthur told the House subcommittee,

"Within five to ten years it would be possible to make a new infective microorganism which would differ in certain important aspects from any known disease-causing organisms. Most important of these is that it might be refractory to the immunological and therapeutic processes upon which we depend to maintain our relative freedom from infectious disease."

MacArthur also reported that,

"Should an enemy develop it there is little doubt that this is an important area of potential military technological inferiority in which there is no adequate research program."

MacArthur received the money that he wanted. By 1971 research into "hazardous viruses" was underway at Fort Detrick. If it is a coincidence that AIDS, a disease that matches the characteristics of the "new infective microorganism," appeared within the "five to ten years" time frame stipulated by MacArthur, then it is a truly amazing coincidence.

In November of 1978 over a thousand male homosexuals were given experimental vaccinations for hepatitis B by the National Institutes of Health and the Center for Disease Control. Was it just a coincidence that six years later 64 percent of the subjects of the test had AIDS?

It is also important to note that the hepatitis B vaccine alleged to have infected the gay men was probably manufactured by the company owned by George Merck, the man who had headed the American agency on biowarfare during World War II. According to a report in the *New England Journal of Medicine*,

"The vaccine was prepared in the laboratories of the Department of Virus and Cell Biology Research, Merck Institute for Therapeutic Research, West Point, PA... The vaccine, made from the plasma of HBsAg [hepatitis B surface antigen] carriers... was treated... A large number and variety of tests were carried out by the manufacturer on the initial plasma pools, the antigen concentrates, and the vaccine to insure microbial sterility and the absence of extraneous viruses. The vaccine was also tested for live hepatitis A virus (HAV) in marmosets [a type of monkey] and live HBV [hepatitis B virus] in susceptible chimpanzees."

The connection is never made in the media between AIDS and the fact that vaccines sometimes become contaminated with monkey viruses. For instance, *The New York Times* on July 26, 1961 reported that vaccine manufacturer Parke-Davis had determined to quit distributing their Salk vaccines "until they can eliminate a monkey virus." Still, there is no connection made to the most famous alleged monkey virus of all time.

A doctor of bacteriology, Bernice Eddy, discovered live monkey viruses in Salk polio vaccines in 1954. She testified before a U.S. Senate Investigation in 1971 that unless problems with the contamination of vaccines was dealt with, slow monkey viruses would set off human cancer epidemics internationally. The upshot of Eddy's discovery was that her funding was withdrawn, and her career was destroyed.

Another fascinating thread to pull in the question of AIDS as biowarfare is the connection of Dr. Robert Gallo, the man heralded as having discovered the virus that causes AIDS. Gallo, before his reported discovery, had in fact been involved in the creation of many AIDS-like viruses in the laboratory. By 1972 Gallo's research group was involved in injecting ribonucleic acid from one type of virus into another to create mutants that, according to Dr. Leonard Horowitz, "functioned just like the AIDS virus."

Among the types of research conducted by Gallo was the modification of simian monkey viruses through the infusion of cat leukemia RNA to create cancers of the sort observed in persons with AIDS, and the cloning of monkey viruses. In 1969 or 1970 Gallo and fellow researcher Seitoku Fujioka indicated that they need to "evaluate the functional significance of tRNA changes in tumor cells." They formulated an experiment in which "specific tumor cell tRNAs" were "added directly to normal cells." Viruses used were the simian monkey virus (SV40) and the mouse parotid tumor. According to Dr. Leonard Horowitz, "These experiments, I realized, could have easily established the technology for the development of HIV—allegedly of simian virus descent..."

And what was the source of Gallo's funding during this period? Among others, Gallo worked with Litton Bionetics, Inc., a company linked to biological warfare research, that had been inoculating simian monkeys with mutant viruses since 1962.

The parent company of Litton Bionetics is Litton Industries, whose president at the time, Roy Ash, was one of three alternate appointees for Henry Kissinger for the head of the National Security Council, six months prior to Congress being asked by the Department of Defense to fund experimentation with AIDS-like viruses. According to Dr. Leonard Horowitz, Gallo received support "from at least a third of the Army's top eighteen biological research contractors, including Bionetics, Hazelton, the University of Chicago, Stanford University, Dow Chemical, and New England Nuclear Corp..."

According to Randy Shilts in *And the Band Played On*, his chronicle of research into the origin of AIDS, Gallo engaged in efforts that Shilts interprets as sabotaging international efforts to isolate the AIDS retrovirus. Among other activities, Gallo is alleged to have withheld from researchers antibodies required to identify AIDS-like viruses. Was this simply an example of proprietary approach to the research, or was it indeed an attempt to stop the research?

Researcher Dr. Leonard Horowitz wonders, "Had Gallo been ashamed of creating the virus years earlier, so he tried to block its discovery, terrified it might be traced to BW research?"

The preponderance of evidence shows that the AIDS virus was man-made. But was the massive worldwide plague that has resulted from its release intentional or accidental?

According to Dr. Frederick Rasmussen, Jr. of the University of California School of Medicine—incidentally a biowarfare weapons contractor—has warned that mass vaccination programs could, in themselves, result in AIDS-like diseases, through the alteration of the host's immune system:

"In view of the complexity and diversity of immunizing antigens and the possible host responses, an occasional adverse interaction should not surprise us. Such proved, widely-used vaccines as pertussis and BCG are known to increase and modify immunological reactivity profoundly. A number of viral immunogens, notably measles, consist of or are prepared from viruses... There must also be biological interactions, genetic among sufficiently closely related viruses and through sharing of virus coded mechanisms for the synthesis of subunits [viral components and newly-produced viruses].

"The dangers confronting us in the development and use of new vaccines, together with those known to exist with the present vaccines, may have been overemphasized, but they are very real..."

Rasmussen added,

"Among the dangers... the possible potentiation or activation of certain slowly progressive viral infections is particularly difficult to combat, because untoward reactions may be so few or so distantly related to the initiating immunizing procedure as to be overlooked unless rigorous and sustained surveillance is undertaken—and, even if recognized, may not become clearly evident until large numbers of people have been placed at irreversible risk.

"If we are to anticipate unknown dangers it is imperative that all facets of the immune response and other host responses to any new product be exhaustively studied..."

If the release of AIDS was intentional, who was responsible, and what was their purpose?

The most obvious culprit would be the American military. Supporting the idea that the AIDS virus may have been used to intentionally contaminate hepatitis B vaccine is that biowarfare research is deliberately compartmented. According to CIA Director William Colby, testifying before a Select Committee to Study Governmental Operations with Respect to Intelligence Activities, on September 16, 1975,

"If the particular activity is a very sensitive matter and only a very few employees need to know it, then it will be known to only a very few employees. We make a particular effort to keep the identities of our sources and some of our complicated technical systems restricted very sharply to the people who actually need to work on them. And many of the rest of the people in the Agency know nothing about them."

The CIA has a long history of working in Africa under the cover of other agencies. These have included AFRICARE, CARE, the CDC, the Peace Corps, PUSH (People to Save Humanity), the Rockefeller and Ford Foundations, USAID, the World Bank, the World Health Organization, even NASA and the National Academy of Sciences.

Another possibility, suggested by Dr. Robert Strecker, is that a hostile foreign party might be responsible.

One connection of extreme interest was revealed by Soviet press official Boris Belitsky in an interview on the *Moscow World Service* radio network. Asked about new information suggesting that AIDS was a man-made virus, Belitsky
replied:

BELITSKY: Just recently a Soviet journalist in Algeria,
Aleksandr Zhukov, managed to interview a European physician at the Moustapha Hospital there, who made some rel-
evant disclosures on the subject. In the early seventies, this
physician and immunologist was working for the West German OTRAG Corporation (Orbital Transport and Missiles,
Ltd.) in Zaire. His laboratory had been given the assignment
to cultivate viruses ordinarily affecting only animals but con-
stituting a potential danger to man. They were particularly
interested in certain unknown viruses isolated from the African green monkey, and capable of such rapid replication that
they could completely destabilize the immune system. These
viruses, however, were quite harmless for human beings and
the lab's assignment was to develop a mutant virus that would
be a human killer.

HOST: Did they succeed?

BELITSKY: To a large extent, yes. But when they inoculated the inhabitants of several jungle villages with such a
mutant virus on the pretext of giving shots against cholera,
this did not produce the immediate results required of the
lab. Now, it is well-known that people infected with AIDS
virus can live for several years without developing the disease but at the same time the result was summed up as proving the unsuitability of the virus as a biological warfare agent.
The lab was ordered to wind up the project and turn the results over to certain U.S. researchers who had been following this work with keen interest, to such an extent that some
of the researchers believed they were in reality working not
for the West German OTRAG Corporation but for the Pentagon. In fact, two U.S. assistants had been with the lab
throughout the work on this project. Several years after the
lab had turned over its findings to the Americans, back came

the news of the first AIDS cases in San Francisco. The researcher believes that the Pentagon had tested the mutant virus on convicts in California.

The OTRAG organization is like something out of a James Bond novel, although the company is perfectly real. Ostensibly a private enterprise in the business of developing inexpensive satellite-launching missiles, an investigation by the German Information Service of South Africa has revealed that the company was subsidized by the West German government. Researcher Tad Szulc, citing secret service sources, has said that OTRAG is an arm of West Germany's Dornier and Messerschmidt munitions companies and has implicated the United States in engaging in a nuclear weapons development program with OTRAG. Another report from a CIA agent to a British journalist states that Boeing Company had given OTRAG access to sophisticated Cruise missile technology.

Key OTRAG personnel have also been traced to the Third Reich. Examples of this include:

— The founder and manager of OTRAG was Lutz Thilo Kayser. He had been a special advisor to the Minister of Research and Technology of West Germany, and on the ad hoc committee on the Apollo program transport systems. In World War II Kayser was allegedly known as "Dadieu's young man," referring to his mentor Armin Dadieu, a high-ranking SS officer.

— Kurt H. Debus, Chairman of the Board of OTRAG in the 1970s, was a former director of the Cape Canaveral space research program. During World War II, however, Debus is alleged to have worked on the German V2 missile program at Peenemunde, Germany.

— Eugen Sanger and Wolf Pilz, two rocket scientists from Peenemunde.

In the 1970s, OTRAG contracted with the government of Zaire for the "unlimited use" of nearly 100,000 square kilometers of the country until the year 2000. Although this territory has 760,000 people inhabiting it, OTRAG has complete control over it and its air space, with complete immunity from the laws of Zaire. It is also noteworthy that the OTRAG project is located in Shaba, which is a center of CIA black operations.

A number of countries including the Soviet Union, East Germany, Yugoslavia and Cuba have protested the Zaire OTRAG project, stating that West Germany is using it as a pretext for offensive missile development to bypass restrictions on the country in the 1954 Brussels Treaty. Other sources have said that the U.S. and France were also involved in the project.

Assessing the above information, the idea that OTRAG may have been used as a cover for covert research and production of biowarfare is also quite plausible.

I don't subscribe to the theory of some researchers that AIDS was unleashed as a depopulation measure, to reduce the number of people in the world. Although I am well aware that the elite of the world do believe that there are too many people—that fact has come forward in the statements of many elite planners—it seems exceedingly unlikely that they would launch a virus that could potentially take themselves and their own families.

But, these same theorists suggest, the elite must have developed a vaccine or other curative means to proof themselves against AIDS. Fortunately, although there are numerous experimental regimens for curing AIDS, with some of them showing promise, there is nothing to suggest such a program exists at this time. The most probable answer is that the AIDS plague is the result of an accidental escape of the virus from an experimental lab, probably one researching biological warfare.

# 1 3

## OUTBREAKS

**B**etween July and November 1976 there were two almost simultaneous disease outbreaks of ebola disease about 1000 kilometers apart in Southern Sudan and northern Zaire. There were over 500 cases in the two locations, with almost 400 deaths, although it is acknowledged that these figures may have been low estimates.

The first cases of ebola appeared in the Sudan, where the source of the infections was not determined. Within two months there was another outbreak in Zaire, where it is believed that hypodermic injections given in a hospital "played a role" in transmission.

At this time there is no cure for ebola, nor is there any particular treatment. The effects of ebola are gruesome. Within days, the temperature goes through the roof of those infected. They suffer horrible pain in the muscles and joints. It becomes impossible to swallow. The skin has been described as turning into something like soft bread with blood oozing out. The body bleeds from every orifice, and the victims inhale the surfaces of their own tongues and throat. Finally the victims go into convulsions, thrashing around in agony in their own blood until they die.

Ebola reappeared in 1995, beginning with a patient at a hospital in Kikwit, Zaire. The virus spread to hospital staff, and from there to other areas of the country. Dr. Leonard Horowitz comments on one unusual aspect of the disease:

"Indeed it was hard to believe that Ebola Zaire, which had differentiated itself genetically from its predecessor, Ebola Sudan, over the course of five months and 500 miles, had emerged almost twenty years later, over the same distance, virtually unaltered. Some believe that modern technology may have helped, that is, refrigeration."

A bestselling book was released about the ebola outbreaks, *The Hot Zone* by Richard Preston. This book, amazingly, entirely avoided the possibility that ebola may have been a man-made virus. But, certainly, there may have been a method to the madness.

A *New York Times* article titled "Grants by Foundations Help Technology Books Make It to the Shelves" revealed that Preston had received a sizeable grant from the Sloan Foundation, "though the book did not fit into the Sloan technology series." Is it possible that Preston's funding might have dictated the slant of his book?

The Sloan Foundation, according to Dr. Leonard Horowitz, "supported black educational initiatives consistent with the COINTELPRO Black Nationalist Hate Group campaign" and "administered mass-media-public-persuasion experiments completely consistent with the CIA's Project MKULTRA—efforts to develop brainwashing technologies and drugs to affect large populations..." Sloan also funded studies of population limitation by Planned Parenthood-World Population, provided over $200,000 yearly to the Council on Foreign Relations.

Hantavirus was first noted as causing illness in GIs during the Korean War, with a 5-10% mortality rate among those who contracted the disease. Although the virus was detected in rats in the Orient and in the United States, it was little noticed until an outbreak of hantavirus among mostly Native Americans in the "Four Corners" area of the Southwestern United States in 1993; this time the mortality rate for some reason had increased to 60%. The outbreak was attributed to infected deer mice.

But there is another common factor in both the hantavirus outbreaks: the U.S. military. Here are the smoking guns that suggest that hantavirus may have originated as a manufactured biowarfare weapon:

(1) It has been reliably confirmed that the army used biowarfare weapons in Korea.

(2) The Four Corners area where hantavirus reappeared in 1993 is only a few miles from Fort Wingate, a U.S. Army biowarfare experimentation center, that had only been decommissioned a few months prior.

The following information was reportedly provided by a formerly high ranking U.S. Intelligence officer to RMNews Agency:

"Operation Rain Dance was called to life by the Department of the U.S. Army, an Air Force Special Research Unit, and Bio Medics from the U.S. Navy. It was officially born in the first quarter of 1989 and held one purpose in common; how to eradicate one special race of people. (Through manipulation of genes any race of people could be the target group.)

"The project was called LVNM Special Labs Division. It was located at an insane asylum in Las Vegas, New Mexico. (That's where the LVNM comes from). It also bore a code signal, SB-17.

"SB-17 was a virus they were working on to target and kill only Native Americans. This fact was clearly detailed through the ops file, and ops memo to the Pentagon Special Projects Division.

"Desert rats were used to carry the virus into towns and municipalities. There the virus was transmitted via fecal matter into the local water supply, and broken down, bacteriologically, it was able to enter the food chain.

"Do you remember the 7-9 Navajo Indians who died of mysterious circumstances? The coroner's report was "death induced by unknown virus." The experiment was a success. Only American Indians died of the virus. (Hanta?)

"The Pentagon recalled its Special Projects Team and cleaned up the entire area of about 50 square miles. All they had to do was spray the affected area from their black helicopters, and the dying ceased.

"Now, they are in possession of a weapon far more deadly than any gas or other chemical weapon. With minor alterations, this virus could be used against any race of people and it would cause death within 5 days.

"The E-Coli bacteria is also out of labs in Ft. Meade. It also kills. All they have to do is alter its strain, and many, many people could die of it. With E-Coli they can also determine its death point, as far as temperatures are concerned. There are 65 of these "animals" ready to set loose upon mankind. Their symptoms appear very natural and are not traceable on any analyzer."

In August of 1967 a hitherto-unknown hemorrhagic fever appeared simultaneously in Germany and Yugoslavia. Thirty-one persons were infected, and seven cases resulted in death. The virus was reportedly traced to shipments of 500-600 monkeys that had arrived from Uganda, although curiously shipments of the monkeys had also been sent to at least five other countries where outbreaks did not occur. An investigation in Africa did not turn up any cases of the disease, causing experts to conclude that the source of what would come to be called the Marburg virus was in Africa, in the animals' native habitat.

Not everyone agreed with that assessment. As Dr. Seymour Kalter, one of the world's experts in simian virology, stated at a Frederick Cancer Research Center symposium in 1975:

"For the sake of completeness, we might mention one or two other points that are important to the total picture. I'll address myself principally to some of the viral diseases. We just referred to Marburg. I believe simian-hermorrhagic fever is important. It appears to be a man-made disease."

At the conference, Kalter was rebutted by Alfred Hellman from the National Cancer Institute, defending the 'official' position that the Marburg virus had migrated 'horizontally' from apes to man. Hellman said,

"In regards to what Sy Kalter was saying about the RNA tumor viruses, reports have appeared in recent newspaper articles, for example *The Times*, on the isolation of a virus from a woman with myelogenous leukemia. Thus far the immunology and some of the hybridization biochemistry data on this virus would suggest that it has some relation, if not a lot of relation, with the Wooly and Gibbon agents which cause a malignancy in these animals. Apparently at least from the data... it appears that the Gibbon ape lymphosarcoma virus probably is transmissible horizontally. I believe one should be aware of this and concerned about the possible relationship of these agents with that isolated from a human."

But how could two experts in the field have such widely differing beliefs about the 'horizontal' transmission of the Marburg virus to humans? Perhaps the interests of deniability dictated at least one conclusion. Hellman at the time was the chairman of the National Cancer Institute's department of Biohazards Control and Containment. He was also the executive in charge of a joint Navy/NCI project on "Aerosol Properties of Potentially Oncongenic Viruses." Hellman also allegedly oversaw a program in which American servicemen were exposed to cancer causing agents. Naturally, the identities of the servicemen were kept secret.

A study by the Center for Disease Control seemed to show that the Marburg virus was a common infection among monkeys worldwide, but these findings were disputed by numerous studies by other experts. Subsequent research showed that the CDC tests were false positives. Had there been an innocent mistake by the CDC, or had the findings been purposely falsified to throw researchers off the actual trail to the source of the Marburg virus?

# 1 4

## TERRORISTS

Amongst many disturbing trends, there is another one. That is in the acquisition of CBW weapons by political revolutionary groups, religious extremist groups, and ethnic separatist factions. Groups such as these are not likely to have ethical qualms or to fear retaliation, since they are often acting on direct orders from God. In recent years the threat of attacks from this quarter has greatly increased, and incidents of the use of CBW weapons by such groups occur in increasing numbers.

Offering an easy opportunity for small revolutionary groups to obtain chemical and biological weapons, formulas for creating even the most potent weapons can be found in scientific texts available in any university library. Additionally, many of the elements needed to produce CBW weapons (including smallpox, plague, brucellosis, and tularemia) can be obtained from easily-obtained natural sources. Corn can be used for obtaining tricothecene mycotoxin, and peanuts can be used to obtain aflatoxin. Ricin toxin can be isolated from easily obtained and cultivated castor beans. Fertilized hen eggs can be used to grow rickettsial and viral agents, and one commentator states that, "theoretically, using a dozen chicken eggs in this fashion, enough psittacosis virus could be produced to infect everyone on earth."

Supplies of deadly biological agents can also be obtained ready-made from medical supply labs. The cost of these agents is for the most part incredibly low, with samples of anthrax bacillus going for as little as $35. It is true that a permit is needed to obtain harmful germ cultures, but this can be obtained fraudulently, as has been demonstrated in many cases in recent years. The only other necessity is a letterhead, real or forged.

According to the World Health Organization, some deadly agents like smallpox virus "can be produced and used as weapons with relatively simple techniques." Another study stated, "To a knowledgeable person the procedures required to obtain strains or cultures of very dangerous toxins and diseases—and to produce them in sufficient quantities—are about as complicated as manufacturing beer and less dangerous than refining heroin."

Another possibility for obtaining bacterial or viral agents is for a graduate to obtain work at a medical lab or research foundation. According to one text, "There would be little problem for a "graduate student" conducting "research" to obtain cultures from a supply house or from other researchers. Culture swapping is a common practice, and largely uncontrolled."

Most biological laboratories have very little in the way of security, and access can often be secured, according to knowledgeable sources, by the simple means of donning a lab coat.

Another way of obtaining biologicals would be to bribe, blackmail, or threaten a doctor or other research personnel. A terrorist hit on most biological labs would meet—rather, has met—with little or no resistance from security forces. These facilities are usually guarded only minimally.

The U.S. government admits that stocks of their extremely potent VX nerve agent are missing, and have been offered in black market sales in New York. Storage dumps for chemical and biological weaponry have been compared in some instances to the security on an average supermarket.

And once chemical or biological agents are in hand, they are simple to culture and store with little fear of detection. Stockpiles of biologicals are easy to disguise, and can also be moved from one location to another with little difficulty. Although we are reminded in the press of the vast biological warfare laboratory facilities that Saddam Hussein is supposed to possess, it is rarely mentioned that sufficient quantities of BW agents can be cultured in standard petri dishes, or even from equipment found in children's chemistry sets.

Among many factors making chemical and biological weaponry attractive to nation states as well as terrorists is that almost all targets, ranging from individuals to nations, are vulnerable to these sorts of weapons.

In 1960, General Marshall Stubbs, head of the U.S. Army Chemical Corps, warned of the potential threat of biological weapons to nation states. He said that using "dry biological material," and using only ten aircraft, an enemy could launch an assault on America that would kill or cripple thirty percent of the country's populace, or seventy million people.

According to *Time Magazine*,

"Officials in Washington are deeply worried about what some of them call 'strategic crime.' By that they mean the merging of the output from a government's arsenals; like Saddam's biological weapons, with a group of semi-independent terrorists, like radical Islamist groups who might slip such bioweapons into the U.S. and use them." This would also have the advantage of providing deniability for the country sponsoring the biological attack.

In an interview with Iraq's Deputy Prime Minister Tariq Azziz, the politician denied that the country would ever engage in any sort of terrorism. "No," he said, "we are not in the business of terrorism. You know that." But he also admitted that there were certain groups who sympathized with Iraq who had no such qualms. "There are," he said, "people in other countries who are not satisfied with the situation about Iraq. If a military attack is waged against Iraq, that will increase the resentment against the Americans, and more people would be in that mood."

The possibility of a terrorist attack is far from simply theoretical; there are already calls from certain quarters for an attack on the U.S. and its interests. According to a *Reuters* report for February 25, 1998,

"Muslim militants have issued an open call for attacks on U.S. civilians and allied interests worldwide, U.S. security officials said... The calls were distributed by a coalition of Islamic groups in London and by Usama Bin Ladin, a Saudi national branded by the State Department as a 'well-known terrorist,' the officials said... Both purported edicts said attacks should continue until U.S. forces 'retreat' from Saudi Arabia and Jerusalem. The one distributed in the names of Islamic groups in Britain also blessed attacks until economic sanctions on Iraq are lifted..."

Two experts on chemical and biological weapons offered the following scenario in their treatment of the subject:

"Terrorists, for example, might outfit an old tanker with internal tanks (suitable for the storage of a chemical or biological agent), powerful pressurized aerosol generators (which could turn the agent into a deadly cloud of vapor), and external booms. From all outward appearances it would look like just another rusting Liberian tanker as it passed through The Narrows heading toward New York. But off the tip of Manhattan it could crank up the generators and open the booms. Within minutes, if weather conditions were right, a great expanding cloud of lethal vapor would be drifting toward the World Trade Center towers. Because the vapor would likely be both odorless and colorless, and thus undetectable to any observer, the ship would be able to dock in New Jersey and the terrorists could escape before the authorities could pinpoint the source of the attack. If the attack was of biological character rather than chemical, it might take days or weeks for the effects to become evident, by which time the terrorists might be halfway around the world."

This scenario parallels actual testing by the U.S. military during the 1950s, when two U.S. minesweepers in the open sea just beyond Golden Gate Bridge were used to spray the bacterial agents Bacillus globigii and Serratia marcescens in a simulation of an attack from a foreign power. Documentation shows that virtually all of the residents of San Francisco at that time inhaled at least five thousand bacterial particles discharged from the vessels. If the bacteria had not been a weakened strain, but had instead been one of the many virulent strains possessed by many nations at this time, seventy-five percent of the population of the city would have come down with the diseases and would have required hospitalization. As many as eighty percent of the hospitalized would have died, according to one estimate.

Another scenario was offered in a National Advisory Committee report of March 2, 1977. The report advised,
"An attacker might simply drive through a medium-sized city using a truck-mounted dispenser. During spring or summer, this type of apparatus would not raise questions in most locales. Anyone exposed for two minutes would probably inhale enough to be infected. Not all the victims would receive lethal doses, but the medical-care problems associated with tens of thousands of cases of anthrax infection in themselves would be catastrophic for a community."

On the other hand, instead of playing "Mission: Impossible," one might just scale a fence and toss vials of biological or chemical agents, say, at a meeting of politicians or industrial leaders. In March, 1976, security at Metropolitan Edison's Three Mile Island nuclear plant were unable to stop "a disturbed former employee who entered the protected area around the utility's nuclear reactor." An electrician who had formerly worked at the facility, drove onto the island, climbed an eight-foot high fence, wandered in the security area for about an hour, and then left.

Unfortunately, although many individuals in government and the military are aware of the threat posed by terrorist groups employing biochemical weapons, there has been little done to prepare for such an eventuality, other than occasional trial runs dramatizing terrorist hits. The Army and Marine Corps have set up task forces to respond to biochemical attacks, but that is about the size of preparations that have taken place. Local authorities usually receive little in the way of responding to such a threat, and hospital personnel are often completely unaware of methods of helping victims of biowarfare attacks. Although antidotes, antibiotics, and other medical supplies should be stockpiled around the country, they are not in any significant quantity.

The situation is remarkably simple: virtually any group desiring deadly chemical or biological agents can readily obtain them. And any group in possession of this kind of weapon has the ability to bring a nation to its knees, if not destroy it entirely.

# 1 5

## CHEMICAL/BIOLOGICAL WARFARE
## AN OVERVIEW

The *Seattle Times* of November 20, 1970 reported that an informant "notified the U.S. Customs Bureau that the revolutionary Weatherman Organization is planning to steal biological weapons from Ft. Detrick, Md., and contaminate a major city's water supply, the Army said yesterday... The informant reported that the Weatherman members plan to obtain the biological materials by blackmailing a homosexual lieutenant at Ft. Detrick, the Army said, confirming an account in Jack Anderson's syndicated column... The plan's aim is to cause havoc, he said, and increase possibilities of revolution."

In January of 1972 in Chicago, the neo-Nazi "Order of the Rising Sun" was arrested in possession of eighty pounds of typhoid bacillus culture that they had manufactured. Their idea, according to the arresting agents, was to drop the typhoid into the water system of several Middle Western cities, including Chicago and St. Louis. The Rising Sun members were supposedly apprehended in a routine traffic stop, and the typhoid culture was discovered in their car.

Although the details are scanty, in 1972 there was an attempt "to use CW [chemical warfare] agents in an attack on a U.S. nuclear storage site in Europe..."

In a strange foreshadowing of the Unabomber case, in 1974 a series of messages was sent to government officials from a man they dubbed "the Alphabet Bomber." He threatened the authorities by saying that he possessed nerve gas and was going to kill the President of the United States. Although most such warnings would be unbelievable, according to those involved in his arrest, the Alphabet Bomber seemed to know what he was talking about when it came to nerve agents. His descriptions were "highly sophisticated. He said all the right things and used the right pronunciations of extremely technical terms."

An intensive manhunt was launched, culminating in the August 1974 arrest of Muharem Kerbogovic, who had moved to the United States from Yugoslavia. Kerbogovic was charged with several bombings in the U.S. He is also said to have sent toxic material to a Supreme Court justice. Some reports say that Kerbogovic was arrested on the afternoon that he was to pick up substances that would have enabled him to complete the compounding of a nerve agent.

Naples, Italy, November, 1974: Forty-eight people, including an official of the Port Agency, were brought to court on charges of being responsible for a cholera outbreak in 1973.

In July of 1976, at an American Legion convention in Philadelphia, 220 people became ill from an unknown cause. Thirty-four of them eventually died.

*U.S. News and World Report*, on September 13, 1976, speculated that "Legionnaires disease" may have actually been a terrorist hit. Columnist Jack Anderson confirmed that Congressional investigators believed that "a demented veteran or paranoid anti-military type" with a knowledge of basic chemistry might have been responsible for the disease outbreak. Anderson quoted America's leading expert on nickel poisoning, who said, "The exposure to nickel carbonyl must have been introduced willfully, because the quantity found in the tissue of the victims could not otherwise be explained."

Anderson also wrote in his column of an anonymous letter sent before the legionnaires' outbreak, that had been mailed before public attention had been focused on the incident. The letter "referred to substances containing nickel carbonyl and discussed the murder and killing of authority and military-type figures."

As the investigation progressed, a previously-unknown bacteria, dubbed Legionella pneumophyla, was found in the hotel's air conditioning system. Suspicions still linger that the infestation may have been done on purpose. It has also been discovered that cases of Legionnaires disease are increasing, with about 10,000 cases of the previously unknown disease diagnosed every year.

A small amount of Chilean-produced sarin, a nerve agent, originally manufactured to be used against Argentina or Peru, was smuggled into the U.S. in 1976 by Michael Townley. It was carried in a Chanel No. 5 atomizer bottle. Its intended use was to assassinate former Chilean Foreign Minister Orlando Letelier.

Also in 1976, a chemical engineer in Vienna manufactured a kilo of a precursor of Sarin. He was arrested after offering to sell it to bank robbers for 14,000 DM.

In late 1976 a quantity of tear gas, stolen from a National Guard armory, was released by an unknown person or persons in San Francisco. At almost the same time the police department of that city reported that a terrorist in possession of a homemade nerve gas had been apprehended.

February 20, 1977: A cloud of poisonous chlorine gas was released from a Dow Chemical plant in Louisiana. Although officials later reported that it had been an accident caused by the rupturing of a storage tank, initial reports by the state police stated that there had been an explosion prior to the release of the gas. Curiously, the plant was only twenty miles away from an Allied Chemical plant where a forty-two mile cloud of chlorine had "leaked" the previous year.

Suggesting that the chlorine expulsion at Dow may not have been an accident, on the same day there was a carbon tetrachloride spill in the Ohio River. The *New York Times* asked, "Who spilled 70 tons of carbon tetrachloride into the Ohio River system, forcing the inhabitants to boil their drinking water two days ago to rid it of the potentially dangerous chemical?" It may be significant that the "spill" had somehow managed to evade the filtration system in Cincinnati.

On June 5, 1977 a reservoir in North Carolina was sabotaged with poison chemicals. Safety mechanisms to prevent the flow of chemicals into the reservoir had been removed and, according to a company official, the perpetrators knew exactly what they were doing.

In 1978 more than a dozen Europeans in at least three countries got sick from eating mercury-contaminated citrus fruit from Israel. In a letter to the Dutch government, the Arab Revolutionary Army Palestinian Commandos claimed credit for the poisoning of the fruit, saying that their purpose was "to sabotage the Israeli economy." Although no one died from the attack, the bottom fell out of Israel's citrus export market for some time after the incident.

In 1978 a terrorist safe house was raided in West Germany. Four hundred kilograms of compounds that could have been used in the production of nerve agents were found.

When the Syrian Embassy in Iraq was searched in August, 1980, explosives, guns, and a vat of poison were discovered.

January, 1981: After being convicted of shoplifting, an angry professor at Towson State University tried to kidnap the store manager who had ordered him to be arrested. The plan didn't work. The professor was arrested and, when police searched his car, they discovered a propane cylinder filled with hydrogen cyanide gas connected to a time release valve.

About two quarts of a tropical fever virus called *chikungunya* disappeared from a laboratory at Fort Detrick, Maryland in September of 1981. Although the scientist who was working with the virus notified his superiors, no investigation took place, and no explanation for the missing viral agent has ever been offered.

The President of the Human Rights Commission of El Salvador was killed in March of 1983. He had been investigating reports of the use of chemical weapons by the El Salvadoran army against civilians.

In May of 1983 it was reported that a plot had been hatched by Israeli Arabs to poison the water in Galilee.

In 1983 a house in Springfield, Massachusetts was raided where two brothers had been manufacturing the potent poison ricin, which is one thousand times more toxic than the government nerve agent VX. The FBI confiscated an ounce of nearly pure ricin in a 35-mm film container and took it to the Army's Ft. Detrick disease laboratories.

In the spring of 1984, two Canadians then in Buffalo, New York, telephoned the American Type Culture Collection (ATCC) in Rockville, Maryland. Pretending to be research microbiologists, they ordered cultures of Clostridium tetain and Clostridium septicum, saying that they were employed by ICM Science. They asked that the cultures be sent by Federal Express to Cheektowaga, New York, and after a money order was received the ATCC sent the cultures. Per routine, a receipt was sent to ICM Science, where it was noticed that there were no employees by the names of the persons who had ordered. The Canadian police were notified, and when a second order was sent by the ATCC the two men who had ordered the cultures were arrested.

September of 1984: A production manager at a nursery in Polk County, Florida contacted the Florida Division of Plant Industry. He had found a leaf-spot problem that, with an investigation by experts, was found to be citrus canker. The plant disease also turned up in twenty other nurseries, but not in Florida citrus groves. A canker emergency was called on Florida agriculture. The deputy administrator of plant protection and quarantine at the Department of Agriculture in Washington, D.C. stated, "There have been suspicions that it was intentionally started but we can't prove that it was. Prior to finding the citrus canker, a woman overheard an individual at a motel making the statement that the industry was going to be in for a big shock. The Office of the Inspector General investigated but never found the woman. They were never able to establish what it meant."

Between September 10 and October 7, 1984, in the town of The Dalles in north-central Oregon, 750 people became ill, with 45 hospitalized from salmonella poisoning. The source of the salmonella outbreak was pinpointed by the Oregon State Health Division and the Center for Disease Control as contamination in salad bars. The FBI was satisfied that this was not a case of deliberately instigated poisoning, and closed its investigation of the incident.

A year later David Knapp, a one-time mayor of the Rajneeshpuram religious commune, and a follower of Bhagwan Shree Rajneesh, came forward to tell the story of what had really happened. Knapp recalled that a meeting that took place in July 1984 between himself, other members of the Wasco County, Oregon commune, and Ma Anand Sheela, the Bhagwan's personal secretary. The purpose of the meeting was to figure out ways of influencing the upcoming elections in Wasco County. A number of ways were suggested for limiting voter turnout, including spreading oil on the roads in the county to make driving impossible and creating an electrical blackout so that alarm clocks would fail.

Finally, the method was hit upon: germs. Ma Anand Puja, the head of the medical clinic at the commune, recommended the use of salmonella, and cultures were purchased from a lab in Seattle. This was easy, since there was a state-certified medical laboratory at the commune. After at least two failed trial runs in which no one became ill, Ava Avalos, one of the members of the commune drove to The Dalles and squirted salmonella bacteria into coffee creamers and salad dressings at ten restaurants. An estimated 751 persons became ill.

On July 22, 1986 Ma Anand Sheela was sentenced to jail for four-and-a-half years for the poisoning and other federal charges.

On October 14, 1984, a revolutionary Red Army Faction safe house was raided by the Paris police. In the RAF flat were found pages of information on bacterial pathology with marginal notes said to have been made by Silke Maier-Witt, a medical assistant who was also apparently a member of the RAF. Other items found in the apartment were medical publications dealing with bacterial infection, forged documents including passports, printing presses, and bomb-making instructions. In the bathroom was a bathtub filled with flasks of Clostridium botulinum.

In the U.S. in 1984, bottles of Tylenol in drug and grocery stores were contaminated with arsenic, resulting in several deaths.

— 1985: The coffee in an Israeli military mess hall was contaminated with carbamate nerve agent. The source of the contamination is not known.

In 1985, soft drink and milk containers in the United States were contaminated by paraquate.

In 1985, again, bottles of Tylenol were contaminated with poison in the U.S. An anonymous report from a worker at a Tylenol plant said that the poisoning actually came from chemical contamination at the plant, and that the "terrorist" story was a cover-up, but this rumor has not been confirmed.

Also in 1985, a group of neo-Nazis was arrested in the United States. They were in possession of thirty gallons of cyanide, and had reportedly planned to dump the poison into the water systems of New York City and Washington, D.C.

*Strategic Forum*, published by the National Defense University, in April of 1990 reported that members of the Japanese *Aum Shinri Kyo* ("Supreme Truth Sect") apocalyptic religious sect rigged three trucks to expel botulin toxin from its exhaust. The auto was then driven around the parliament building in Tokyo. After that the trucks drove to the U.S. Navy installation at Yokohama and sprayed in that area. No one became ill at either location, apparently due to the weakness or the dispersion of the toxin.

In early June 1993, a car was used to spread botulinum toxin in Tokyo during the wedding of Prince Naruhito, Japan's Crown Prince. ["The Threat of Bioterrorism"]

In late June, 1993, a sprayer system was installed on the roof of an Aum-owned building in Tokyo. For four days, a slurry of liquid anthrax was spewed into the air of the city by the sprayer. They tried again in July, driving a truck around the Legislature building in Tokyo. Again, no one got sick from the attack.

An unexplained chemical leak believed to be sarin in the central Japanese town of Matsumoto in June of 1994 killed eight and hospitalized 212. At the time, authorities did not know the source of the poisoning.

On March 5, 1995, 19 train passengers in Yokohama, Japan were hospitalized with eye irritation and respiratory problems; the source of the problems was not determined.

On March 15, three brief cases were found at a subway station in Tokyo. Each concealed containers of an unknown liquid that was to be dispersed by small fans in the briefcases. One of the cases was reported to already be dispersing the fumes at the time.

Five days later, again in the Tokyo subway system, packages were left behind that began emitting a poisonous gas that turned the subway into a scene of turmoil. People collapsed unconscious while thousands of subway riders fled the underground system. In the aftermath of the chemical attack, 12 people had been killed and 5,500 were injured.

By March 22, 1995, the Tokyo police and the Japanese military thought they had found the culprits for the attacks. A task force of 1,200 men raided properties fifty miles west of Tokyo. The location was known to be where mystical guru Shoko Asahara's *Aum Shinrikyo* religious group lived. Police cut their way into an *Aum* warehouse with power saws and acetylene torches. They carried caged canaries to detect poison gases. The police discovered a stockpile of over a hundred tons of chemicals that the authorities claimed could have been used in the production of chemical weapons, although spokespersons for the sect claimed they had been used in manufacturing. Although authorities stated that the chemicals could have been used as precursors in making sarin, they were unable to produce evidence proving that the chemical itself had actually been manufactured.

Also found on March 22, was a woman who had apparently been confined at a cult facility from December 1994, and who had been anesthetized and beaten after she had revealed plans to leave the group. At about the same time, another cult member who had planned to leave the group was found in a comatose state from having been drugged for weeks. Three doctors for the sect were arrested on charges of illegal confinement. Over 100 members of the sect were arrested on a variety of charges.

The *Aum* group, started in 1989, at the time of the arrest had approximately 10,000 followers in Japan, and according to one report, 30,000 members in Russia. The group had assets estimated to be in the $29 million range. During a raid on another of the group's properties, $8.13 million in cash, ten bars of gold, and a large Soviet-manufactured helicopter were confiscated.

The guru, Shoko Asahara, who had disappeared and remained in hiding, claimed in a video message that it was a frame-up from a rival Buddhist group, but a defector from the *Aum* group told police that members of the group had taken 25,000 plastic bags filled with sarin to a secret location in Japan's Southern Alps in August.

Asahara blamed the United States on doing some chemical biological warfare of their own. He said that, "I am seriously sick. Some fifty percent of my 1,700 pupils are troubled with sickness... The gas was sprayed by U.S. troops, unmistakably." Asahara stipulated that the sickness was Q-fever rickettsia, and that the group had also suffered from sarin and yperite poisoning after U.S. Air Force jets had flown in formation over an *Aum* compound.

On April 7, police found chemical residue of methylphosphon acid monoisopropyl at one *Aum* facility. That chemical is created when sarin decomposes, thus, they claimed, proving that sarin had been present at the location. It was later reported that in 1995 *Aum Shinrikyo* had been trying to develop the gruesome ebola virus as a weapon. Members of the *Aum* group including Asahara himself had travelled to Zaire in 1992 with the stated purpose of helping ebola victims. They were apparently there to obtain ebola samples. Records were also obtained from the group showing that they had purchased quantities of Clostridium botulinum, a biowarfare agent stockpiled by the CIA.

In early April of 1995, again, gas spread through the Yokahama subway station, and 500 persons were hospitalized with eye irritation, dizziness, and coughing.

On April 17, according to the Tokyo Broadcasting System, orders from Shoko Asahara for sect members to make sarin were found in a journal of the "Science and Technology Ministry" of the group. The journal quoted Asahara as saying, "Making sarin is a very hazardous undertaking. When carrying this out, you need much courage."

The gas attack scenario was once again repeated on April 21, 1995, this time on a Yokohama shopping mall. Twenty-four persons were hospitalized.

In April of 1995, a variety of agencies including FEMA, the FBI, the Department of Defense, and the Public Health Service dispatched personnel to Disneyland in California in response to the threat of a nerve gas attack on the amusement park. A few days later, the Baltimore *Sun*, quoting anonymous federal officials, reported that American authorities had detained two Japanese men at the Los Angeles International Airport carrying instructions for making sarin nerve gas, and that they had been members of the *Aum* Shinrikyo ("Supreme Truth") group allegedly responsible for gas attacks in Japan. This report was later denied by the Justice Department, which has stated that the threatened gassing was a hoax.

On May 5, 1995, subway station workers in Tokyo found two bags of burning chemicals in a rest room. It was reported that if the bags had not been extinguished, cyanide gas sufficient to kill 10,000 people would have been dispersed throughout the subway system.

On April 23, Hideo Murai, the second highest official and the head of the Science and Technology unit of the *Aum* sect, was stabbed to death by a "lone assassin" outside the group's Tokyo headquarters. The attacker, identified as Yuko Jo, surrendered to the police. The man was reported to be of Korean descent and a member of "an ultra-nationalist group in Mie, central Japan." *Reuters News Agency* reported, "Asked about the motive for the attack, Joyu said it was too early to say whether it was based on the attacker's personal feelings or instructions from someone else" and "Police said the address Murai's killer gave for where he lived belonged to a Yakuza or Japanese gangster group."

It would not remain a mystery long as to whether Yuko Jo had acted alone in the murder of Hideo Murai. On May 11 Japanese arrested Kenji Kamimine, "a member of Japan's largest underworld group," as an accomplice in the murder.

In April, a book authored by *Aum* leader Shoko Asahara was released in Japan. Asahara wrote of his suffering from "heart disease and cerebral thrombosis," and made the prediction that World War II would start in 1997. Asahara claimed to have found this out from time travelling to the year 2006, where he spoke to survivors of the war.

On May 16, 1995, Japanese authorities arrested Shoko Asahara at a sect building in the farming village of Kamiku Isshiki. Asahara claimed that he was innocent, but witnesses in the group implicated him in the crimes. On June 6, 1995, he was charged with murder for his participation in the subway gassing.

Of decided interest in the *Aum* case is the Russian connection. The sect boasts 30,000 members in Russia. According to a Japanese news agency, the sect tried to buy guns and tanks from "Russian connections," and made guns from parts bought in Russia. In April of 1994, the sect also purchased a helicopter in Russia for $950,000. Russian engineers had also visited sect locations in September of 1994, reportedly to modify the helicopter.

Two members of the *Aum* security organization had previously been employed by the Russian KGB. One had been a colonel, the other a lieutenant colonel. Shoko Asahara had travelled to Russia in 1992, and presumably due to his ability to hand out bribes had quickly been allowed to set up a radio station broadcasting his apocalyptic views, and to quickly acquire a charitable tax status. Asahara was given a multiple-entry visa, allowing free travel in and out of Russia, and while he was there he met with Russian leaders including Alexander Rutskoy and Ruslan Khasbulatov, later linked with the attempted overthrow of Boris Yeltsin.

Asahara's key contact is said to have been Oleg Lovob, a 30-year associate of Boris Yeltsin.

In confessions obtained by the police, it was later revealed that Asahara had planned an "urban guerilla war" in November using gas attacks and assaults by armed squads to bring down the Japanese government.

"If the massive police raids that began on March 22 were delayed until around October, the existence of the Japanese nation would have been in the balance," Home Affairs Minister Hiromu said in an interview.

Stranger and stranger. The following Internet message was reportedly mailed from a CBS radio correspondent identified only as Steven to a writer for the *Tokyo Journal*:

"Been meaning to phone you for some time (I enjoy your column in *Tokyo Journal*). The most interesting aspect of this story is how the Japanese media is NOT reporting the following:

Police requested a large number of gas masks BEFORE the subway attack (Mainichi Shimbun only reported this as far as I've seen);

Secret training in gas mask use the day before the gas attack;

Unusually large number of police inside and outside subway stations very early Monday morning hours before the gas attack;

Squabble between SDF and NPA about using troops in the raid;

Japanese intelligence knew that Aum had facilities to make sarin.

I'm aware that most of the Japanese press has this info but have been told not to release it. What I can't find out is who is putting the major kabosh on it. As far as I know elements of the above have been reported by *CBS Radio*, *London Sunday Times*, *Washington Post* and AP but the Japanese press won't even quote these reports as they usually do when something is too sensitive for them to report directly. This is the biggest case of Japanese media censorship I've seen since first coming here in '81. By the way, I'm covering the story for *CBS Radio*."

In 1992 members of the Los Angeles County Commission for Women's Ritual Abuse Task Force investigating satanic cult activity unexplainably became sick. Although the

*Los Angeles Times* had a field day making fun of the story, claiming that the illnesses stemmed from paranoia, blood tests showed that members of the group had been poisoned.

In a written rebuttal to the *Times* account, Dr. Catherine Gould, chairperson of the task force, said, "In January of 1992 I became aware of a strange pattern of illnesses [affecting] both Los Angeles therapists treating ritual abuse patients, and individuals engaged in support and advocacy work on behalf of ritually abused children and adults."

Among the symptoms that Dr. Gould cited were numbness in the face and extremities, body tremors, weakness, and memory loss. The first person complaining of the symptoms consulted a doctor and was diagnosed as suffering from diazinon poisoning. Diazinon is an organophosphate. Other members of the task force were also diagnosed independently, with the same conclusion drawn: organophosphate poisoning.

In 1994 eighteen residents of Montana were sickened with E. coli bacteria after eating at a Jack-in-the-Box restaurant. This could easily have been ascribed to undercooked meat or a similar cause, except that the strain of E. coli was type 0104:H21, the first instance of its type encountered. All other known E. coli infections have been cause by type 0157:H7. A search for the source of the bacteria was inconclusive, supporting the theory that the Montana sickness may have caused by a purposefully-manufactured E. coli strain, and that it was a dry-run for a potential future terrorist attack.

According to the Americans for Sane Policies Newsletter, eight chemical bombs manufactured by the Soviets were shipped to Cuba by the Angolan government in 1995. A source in the government of Peru stated that after the bombs were shipped from Cuba, they were transported to agents of the Maoist Shining Path terrorist group in Peru. According to the same report, if one of these bombs had been detonated in a city, there was the potential for hundreds of thousands of deaths.

On May 5, 1995, Ohio laboratory technician Larry Wayne Harris, allegedly only certified to check for water purity, and said to have formerly been a member of the white separatist Aryan Nations, used his Mastercard to order bubonic plague bacteria from American Type Culture Collection, in Rockville, Maryland. Harris received three vials of the germs in the mail. According to a search warrant, Harris had wanted to conduct research to counteract the threat of Iraqi rats carrying germs. The man pleaded guilty to a charge of wire fraud in the purchase of the bacteria, and was sentenced to 200 hours of community service and 18 months of probation.

This was not the last that would be heard of Larry Wayne Harris. Wednesday, February 18th, 1998, Americans were startled to hear on the evening news that a "deadly terrorist plot" had been foiled. The Air Force, the Army, and the FBI had swooped in and arrested Harris and William Job Leavitt, Jr., at a Las Vegas office complex. They confiscated a white styrofoam cooler, eight to ten black flight bags labelled BIO-LOGICAL, forty petri dishes, and a Mercedes sedan.

President Clinton and Attorney General Janet Reno commented publicly on the efforts of the FBI that resulted in the capture of American terrorists Larry Wayne Harris and William Job Leavitt Jr., in Henderson, Nevada. A criminal complaint issued by FBI Special Agent John J. Hawken claimed that those men had "knowingly conspired to possess" anthrax, in the form of eight to ten bags of anthrax spores, for use as a weapon.

Harris had been under a federal order prohibiting him from obtaining or conducting experiments with "diseases, bacteria, or germs," the order in response to his arrest in 1995. The complaint that was filed against the two men also noted that the previous summer Harris had told a group of people that he was going to release bubonic plague into the New York subway system. Perhaps significantly, Harris had testified in the criminal case of an acquaintance that he had a "personal involvement with the CIA," although the CIA denied the relationship.

A witness, according to the FBI, reported that Harris had shown him a vial that Harris claimed contained enough anthrax to "wipe out a city. Another man, Ronald G. Rockwell, a felon twice convicted of extortion who characterizes himself as a "cancer researcher," had informed the

FBI that he had "joined Harris and Leavitt in a project to test a device which is supposed to electronically deactivate viruses and bacteria," and that when he was with the two men on February 18, "Leavitt stated that he had 'military grade' anthrax in flight bags in the trunk of his Mercedes-Benz automobile." Apparently Leavitt, an owner of three biological labs, had hired Harris to test the device, based upon the research of the late inventor Royal Rife, that Rockwell was to provided for the sum of $2 million.

Oddly, there had no secrecy involved in negotiations regarding Rockwell's machine, and Leavitt and Rockwell had appeared on the *Lou Epton Show*, a Las Vegas radio talk show, five days before the arrests.

Later reports showed that it had all been a false alarm. On February 24, Harris and Leavitt were cleared of all charges of possessing biological weapons. It turned out that the alleged anthrax spores were vials of anthrax vaccine, according to Harris to be used in experiments in neutralizing anthrax contracted by humans.

Harris had twelve months added to the term of his probation from his 1995 conviction because he is alleged to have violated the probation by telling people that he was associated with the FBI. All charges were dropped against Leavitt, who has no criminal record, and by all accounts is only a concerned citizen interested in researching cures for diseases.

These are the details that the mainstream media came forward with regarding Larry Wayne Harris and William Leavitt, Jr. What the media didn't say is at least as interesting, and potentially far more significant.

Prior to Harris' first arrest for the ordering of bubonic plague bacteria through the mail, the man was studying microbiology at Ohio State University. Harris claims that while studying there he met and became friends with a woman known by the name of Mariam Arif. Arif, Harris says, was from Iraq and was also studying microbiology. She claimed to be related to General Arif, a former president of Iraq, and that a number of her family had been executed by agents of Saddam Hussein.

Harris has said that in February of 1993 Arif confided to him that she had knowledge of an Iraqi project that had put in place at least one hundred eleven person terrorist cells in the United States to release biological weapons simultaneously, focusing on large metropolitan centers. Vials of dehydrated plague and anthrax cultures, Arif maintained, had been brought into this country by Iraqi women, with the vials concealed in their body cavities.

Harris says that Arif told him the biowarfare attacks would take place on Muslim holy days, all of them falling before the year 2002. Also planned to take place at the same time was the destruction of the American power grid by blowing up the nation's major power plants. Harris reports that this information was later confirmed by UN inspection teams in Iraq, and that it was reported on CNN.

Harris says that he contacted numerous government agencies to inform them of the alleged plot, including the FBI and the CDC, but that no one believed what he had to say. After numerous attempts, he was finally debriefed by government officials.

Harris also reports that "undercover black operations men" met with him at his home in Lancaster, Ohio, and he reported that on February 6th and 7th of 1997 they arrested a number of Iraqi women in and around Iowa State University. The women were carrying vials of anthrax or plague virus.

According to Greg Carroll, who interviewed Harris by telephone, "I asked Larry why these fellows would fly that distance to give him this information. He said that they are part of the good faction of the CIA (Those who support the Constitution vs. those who support the tyrannical globalist agenda for a paycheck) and wanted this information to get out to the public so they could take steps to protect themselves from this very real threat to America."

Harris also reports that he was in contact with Ann Johnson, one of the world's foremost experts on anthrax, and that she told him there have been in excess of 15 reports from the CIA and other agencies of Iraqis have bringing anthrax into the U.S. Harris says that Johnson also provided him with information that two Iraqi women were apprehended getting off an airplane in Seattle and, when searched, were found to have vials of anthrax and plague bacteria concealed in their bodies.

Another report that Harris cites was a recent apprehension of Iraqis coming into the United States across the Mexican border, carrying suitcases of plague-infested fleas.

Harris says that an attempt was made on his life in September of 1996, in an attempt to silence him. He has said that he was shot with a needle containing poison. He was sent to the hospital where it was found he had massive blood clots in both lungs. Harris reports that the toxin was analyzed by the CIA and determined to be cobra venom.

It may be important to note that when Harris and Leavitt were arrested traffic was not turned away from the area where they and the supposed anthrax vials were, causing one to wonder if the authorities really did believe they were in possession of such materials.

Although the idea that Harris and Leavitt were planning a terrorist attack turned out to be false, their arrest did pull a tight focus on the possibility of terrorist biowarfare in America. The scenario that Harris alleges, that is, covert Iraqi cells in the United States armed with biowarfare weapons, is not in the least improbable. And if Saddam Hussein has temporarily been put down by American military might, that situation might change if America was destroyed, literally destroyed, by chemical or biological war.

In 1999, a Department of Defense document released under the Freedom of Information Act provided a startling insight into the state of biological warfare research in America. The reprinted document follows, and it deserves to be read carefully:

This document has been cleared by SAF/PA Cleared for limited publication on 29 Dec 97 SAF/PA 97-1104UAV-XA

UAV Technologies and Combat Operations Executive Summary97-1104UAV-XA

US Department of Defense Chemical/Biological Weapons Testing Program

Subject

Use of UAV (Unmanned Aerial Vehicles) as agent/ weapon delivery platforms
Testing Authority
USAF Aeronautical Systems Center, Joint Endurance UAV SPOTier II Plus - Tier III Minus
Testing Location, Unit
USAF Air Combat Command, 11th Reconnaissance Squadron, Nellis AFB, NV
not necessarily limited to Indian Springs area)
Primary Systems Tested
CYPHER UAV, SikorskyUT PREDATOR UAV, General AtomicsOUTRIDER TACTICAL UAV, Alliant Techsystems
Chemical Warfare Agents Tested
Blister Agents — LewisiteNerve agents — Soman, GF, VE, VG, VM, VS, VXVomiting Agents (Riot control) - BromobenzylenanidePsychochemical agents - 3-Quinuelidinyl benzilate Benactyzine
Biological Warfare Agents Tested
Anthrax (Bacillus anthracis)Plague (Yersinis Pestis)Cholera (Vibrio choelerae)Botulism (Clostridium botulinim toxin)Clostridium Perfringens Aflatoxin T-2 trichothcene mycotoxinDAD trichothecene mycotoxinRicin toxinReference: Richard Spertzel, Ph.D.
Lt. Col. Tyle Kanazawa Weapons System Integration DivisionSEAD Conmbat TOS DARPAUAV Joint Task Report SAF/PA 96-1204 UAV
The gist of this report is that the American Department of Defense has been testing chemical and biological weapons using unmanned aerial vehicles at what is popularly known as "Area 51." These craft are what are probably being observed when spectators see "flying saucers" and other unusual aerial objects performing unusual maneuvers in this location.
In recent years, innovations in molecular biology have rendered the weapons of biochemical warfare even more horrifying. Since the 1970s a revolution in biotechnology has

taken place that enables scientists to custom-tailor diseases with specific characteristics and applications, including diseases that cannot be treated using current medical methods. One dirty little secret about biowarfare testing by the U.S. military is the testing of ethnic specific agents. In an Army test in 1951, a disproportionately large number of black persons were exposed to Aspergillus fumigatus. According to an Army report,

"Within this [Naval Supply System] there are employed large numbers of laborers, including many Negroes, whose incapacities would seriously affect the operation of the supply system. Since Negroes are more susceptible to coccidiodes than are whites, this fungus disease was simulated by using Aspergillus fumigatus Mutant C-2."

Another biowarfare weapon experimented with by the Army was the deadly Coccidioides immitis, a fungus found in the soil of the Central Valley in California, in the Southwest, Mexico, and Central America. Even when treated with antibiotics the mortality rate for those who inhale the spores of the fungus is fifty to sixty percent. The fungus is, however, almost entirely ethnic-specific. Twenty to twenty-five percent of infected blacks develop the deadly form of the disease, whereas only one percent of whites do.

Another example of ethnic-specific targeting took place during the Vietnam war, when the Pentagon issued directives to the Advanced Projects Research Agency to "prepare a map portraying the geographic distribution of human blood groups and other inherited blood characters" of the Vietnamese. This project may have been part of the development of a specifically Vietnamese-directed weapon.

Possibly the first time that ethnic-specific weapons were mentioned publicly was in an article published in the *Military Review* for November 1970. This journal is published for military commanders by the U.S. Army Command and General Staff College, located in Fort Leavenworth, Kansas. The article was titled "Ethnic Weapons" and was written by Carl A. Larson, whose credits include running the Department of Human Genetics at the Institute of Genetics, in Lund, Sweden, and who is also a medical doctor. In the article Larson provides a rundown on the advantages of biological weaponry that would specifically target chosen racial groups, in particular those who have not developed nation defenses against certain types of viral or bacterial organisms.

Another government to whom ethnic-specific war weapons was apparently a priority was South Africa. In recent revelations produced by the country's "Truth and Reconciliation" commission, that explored abuses undertaken during apartheid, it was revealed that South African scientists had developed biological and chemical weapons that were used on leaders of the African National Congress, as well as on the population of black townships. These weapons included an infertility toxin that was secretly administered to blacks in order to sterilize them, and poisons that were administered through clothing, as well as in food items and cigarettes.

According to the testimony of President Thabo Mbeki, the apartheid government assassinated "scores" of political opponents through the use of poisons. The South African military is also implicated in the use of poison gas and carcinogens against the blacks, with Nelson Mandela mentioned in a secret memo as being a particular target for the use of carcinogens.

It is noteworthy that the head of the biological warfare program in South Africa has said that the chemical and biological program was specifically aided and encouraged by members of the U.S. military and intelligence agencies.

According to the report of the commission, the white regime in South Africa also injected strains of cholera into the water supplies of some South African villages. Anthrax and cholera bioweapons were used by government troops in Rhodesia in the late 1970s against black rebel forces in the area. In 1979 one of the largest anthrax outbreaks that has ever happened took place in Rhodesia.

General Lothar Neethling, previously employed by the police forensics lab, reported to the commission that he had been ordered to furnish drugs including LSD and Mandrax for use in crowd-control grenades. There was also commission testimony that South African scientists had been working on weapons consisting of bacterial strains that would specifically target blacks.

In Angola, South African forces liaising with members of the U.S. military are circumstantially linked to paralyzing rebel groups with gas attacks, before executing them wholesale.

Israel, according to the *Sunday Times*, in an *Associated Press* release from 1998, has also been actively engaged in developing specifically anti-ethnic weapons. According to that article,

"Israel is trying to identify genes carried only by Arabs that could be used to develop a weapon that would harm Arabs but not Jews, the *Sunday Times* reported. The newspaper attributed its report to unidentified Israeli military and Western intelligence sources. It said Israeli scientists are working to create a genetically modified bacterium that only attacks people who carry certain genes... The newspaper said the program is based at the Biological Institute in Tziyona, which it described as the main research facility for Israel's chemical and biological weapons. According to the report, researchers have pinpointed 'a characteristic in the genetic profile of certain Arab communities, particularly the Iraqi people.'"

Another example of the blatant disregard for human rights is the use of the contraceptive implant called Norplant. Abuses in this area have been so outrageous as to cause us to consider what is supposedly a birth control device as a form of biowarfare against Third World populations. According to Betsy Hartmann, Director of the Population and Development Program at Hampshire College and author of *Reproductive Rights and Wrongs: The Global Politics of Population Control and Contraceptive Choice*,

"Developed by the Population Council in New York, Norplant is a progestin implant system inserted under the skin of a woman's arm, which prevents pregnancy for at least five years. Common side effects of Norplant include menstrual irregularity, headaches, nervousness, nausea, acne and weight gain. Both insertion and removal require local anesthesia and medical skill. Ethical use of the drug depends on adequate medical screening and follow-up, and most importantly on access to removal on demand.

An internal Population Control report provides chilling evidence of how Norplant has been misused in the Indonesian population program. Nearly half a million women have had Norplant inserted, often without counselling them on side effects, alternative contraceptive options, pregnancy screening, and without proper sterilization of equipment. Many of these women have not even been told that the implant must be removed after five years to avoid increased risk of life-threatening ectopic pregnancy.

Moreover, removal on demand is not guaranteed, not only because of lack of trained personnel, but more importantly to serve the government's demographic objectives. According to the Population Council report, "Recent government policy encourages use of Norplant for the duration of the full five years of effectiveness, which is communicated to the client as a form of commitment..." Or as one Indonesian population official put it, "People are told it has to last five years, they give their word...and rural people don't go back on their word. If they request removal, they are reminded that they gave their word."

# 16

## In Harm's Way

A merican officials are beginning to break the bad news to us. They are talking about the danger to America of biological weapons wielded by foreign and domestic terrorist groups. They are not, however, telling us the worst of it.

The proliferation of chemical and biological weaponry on planet Earth threatens the extinction of the human race on this planet. With every two-bit dictator on the planet capable of building up an arsenal of chemical and biological weapons that could kill the entire human population, the prospects are exceedingly grim. And with the advent of designer diseases, a purposeful or accidental release of some potent biowarfare agent would be even more likely to wipe out human life or a significant portion of the human race. The threat to mankind, with the advent of the era of CBW, is far greater than the threat of atomic weapons ever was.

In 1970, the American Nobel laureate Joshua Lederberg said that research into molecular biology "might be exploited for military purposes and result in a biological weapons race whose aim could well become the most efficient means for removing man from the planet."

That is the truth of the matter. Those weapons do currently exist in the arsenals of some countries, will soon be owned by many more, and due to these facts, the potential for the death of humankind as a whole now looms before us.

This is not a Chicken Little scenario that I am talking about. This is not idle talk conceived of to scare the yokels.

Even if chemical and biological weapons do not wipe out mankind from Earth, they may be the catalyst for the virtual atomization of current nation states, fracturing countries into competing regions and shards. Given the inexpensive nature of these CBW agents, the ease in which they are manufactured, and the effectiveness that can be obtained in dispersing them by both terrorist groups as well as militant nation states, there is no limit to the amount of destruction that can be accomplished by this new wave of weaponry.

Think of it this way: Now any country or terrorist group can easily construct weapons that could decimate the most powerful of nations. They can unleash germs that can bring the entire world to its knees.

One particularly devastating possibility has been noted by two Ohio State University veterinarians, John Gordon and Steen Bech-Neilsen, in a paper titled "Biological Terrorism: A Direct Threat to Our Livestock Industry." They conclude that the United States is particularly vulnerable to a biowarfare attack against its livestock, and that diseases such as African swine fever or Newcastle disease, could wipe out the entirety of American meat industry. For the skeptical amongst us, you should remember that there have already been documented cases of apparent biowarfare against food production in America and other countries, as noted in this book.

This is no time for an ostrich-like approach to the problem. The threat of biowarfare in America is not likely to vanish in the near future, if ever. Thus far, incidents of chemical and biological warfare have occurred on a relatively limited basis, but attacks utilizing this kind of weaponry will almost certainly continue to happen, and to escalate in terms of destruction. The dire warnings of people like Larry Wayne Harris, although portrayed by the media as being the fantasy of a fringe crackpot, in all probability will be the reality that we will have to contend with in the future.

Here is the worst of it: we can expect to see a major biowarfare attack on the United States at some time in the near future, particularly if the United States continues its interventionist policy against any nation whose policies do not go along with the plans of the New World Order. The U.S., by interfering in the affairs of other nations, is sowing the seeds of its own destruction.

Whether a major attack comes from an enemy nation state or from an extremist group, it will surely come. The time to make preparations for survival is now.

# Appendix
# In the Event of CBW Attack

Having read the information I have compiled in this book, there is one question that you must ask yourself. What will you do in the event of biowar or a terrorist attack? The answer that you come up with may determine whether you, your friends, or your family survives such an attack.

The author of this book is not a medical doctor or trained in chemistry or medicine, and so the following information should be construed strictly as personal opinion. This book is also not intended to be a highly technical treatise on chemical and biological warfare, but instead an introduction to the subject, primarily to alert people to the fact that there is a chemical/biological threat to the United States. For specific information about the medical aspects and prevention or treatment of the effects of CBW, more technical texts should be consulted.

## INFORMATION

Two references which should provide additional information for those desiring a more technical treatment of the subject are *FOA: A Briefing Book on Biological Weapons*, published by the Swedish National Defense Establishment, and the *U.S. Army Field Manual FM 3-5* (NBC Decontamination), available at some Army surplus stores. Another book providing a good deal of information on types of equipment to be used in the event of CBW attack is *Breath No Evil*, by Stephen Quayle and Duncan Long, published by Safe-Trek Publishing.

A good medical reference book such as *The Columbia University College of Physicians and Surgeons Complete Home Medical Guide* should be a part of your survival stockpile.

## IDENTIFICATION

The state-of-the-art of detection of chemical and biowarfare agents in the air, water, and food of a locality remain primitive. At this time test kits for some specific agents are available, such as the Army Biological Integrated Detection System (BIDS), although it is expected that the U.S. military will be issuing a more comprehensive biowarfare detection kit in the near future. As an example of the state of the art, during the period of the Tokyo *Aum* Shinryko attacks, Japanese police carried cages with canaries, much as miners used to use birds for detecting poisonous gas in mines. Now that I think about it, it might be a good idea to keep a few canaries as pets.

At this time there are a number of chemical agent detectors that vary in effectiveness and in price. A good rundown on these kits can be obtained in *Jane's NBC Protective Equipment*, published by Jane's Information Group.

Some methods of determining a CBW attack are quite obvious:

(1) An alert might be issued in the media, perhaps in lesser known, smaller circulation periodicals, or on the Internet, since the mainstream media has a track record of covering up dangerous situations to the public in order to avoid panic. It is best to have a battery or crank-powered shortwave radio in the event that power goes down, and in order to access news reports from outside of the country in the event of a CBW (or other) attack.

(2) Observable indicators. These might include unusual gaseous clouds, or means of dissemination such as bombs, suitcases, bottles, vials, or other container ejecting gas or spray.

(3) Dead animals or animals exhibiting peculiar behavior in the vicinity.

(4) A verified sudden outbreak of illness, that would not necessarily be identified as chemical or biowarfare in the mainstream media. It is quite possible that in the event of a CBW attack that the media would characterize the attack as a flu or other epidemic to lessen panic.

It is quite possible that in the event of a CBW attack, the warning period in which one had time to prepare would be quite short, even allowing only a matter of minutes. It is best to have access to shelter within minutes of receiving a warning, or seeing signs that a CBW attack is taking place.

It is recommended that in the event of a suspected chemical or biological attack that medical authorities be contacted for advice, if this can be done safely.

## PROTECTION

Although a number of European countries, Switzerland especially, provide civilian shelters, the United States has until now been relatively unresponsive to the threat of CBW attacks. Since it is unlikely that situation will change much in the future, the following are some observations about protecting yourself from CBW weaponry.

## LOCATION

The best protection from chemical or biowarfare threat is to be distant from areas of attack. Ideally, one should be prepared prior to a CBW attack by living in a rural area that might not be targeted because of the lack of population density. Living in a rural area may also buy you time for preparation in the event of a biowarfare disease attack. In other words, get out of the city and into the country, preferably the back country, while you can. Those are the areas where people stand the best chance of surviving, especially if they are prepared to further insulate themselves by isolating themselves from contact with other humans and possibly contaminated food and water sources for a period of time.

The time period during which a CBW attack took place could be days, or it could be years, depending on the circumstance. In a situation of heavy attack with anthrax, for instance, with a possible 'shelf life' of the disease organism consisting of thousands of years, one might wish to drop out from the human race semi-permanently.

If you feel it is impossible to move to the country, then one possibility is to be ready for a quick escape to a more isolated area in the event of CBW attack. You should have food, water, weapons, and shelter in your car, or available at the location you will travel to. At best, this is an iffy proposition, since during a verified CBW attack the roads will probably be clogged with the automobiles of others attempting to escape the city and the highest areas of contamination.

One way of making your chances of survival better is to plan an escape route that would only be accessible by four wheel drive, thus getting the jump on the competition in getting out of a populated area.

If you are in the midst of a city or nearby during an event of CBW attack, there are a few precautions that you can take that will improve the likelihood of your survival:

Have a protected area that can be sealed against a CBW attack. In a building, if the ventilation system is not prepared with filters specifically designed for CBW protection, than the ventilation system should be turned off. Doors, windows, cracks, and other sources of potential air exchange can be sealed off with duct tape, plastic sheeting, aluminum foil, and other non-permeable materials. If possible put several doors and layers of insulation between you and the outside, where the CBW agents will proliferate. The best location against CBW attack is above street level, the higher the better, since CBW agents are heavier than air. Within a house or building, an inner room, without windows, is advisable, or even an insulated area within a room.

An improvised shelter such as described above would not be expected to provide long term protection from CBW agents. A more elaborate shelter would include a High Efficiency Particulate Air filter, available through heating suppliers. These filters are designed to prevent or reduce the flow of bacteria and fungal spores through the heating or air conditioning system in a building.

After an attack, it is best to remain isolated, if possible, from persons who have been infected. If it is impossible to remain isolated from infected persons or areas, then protective clothing and a mask is important. If a person has been identified as a casualty of a biowarfare agent, then they should be kept isolated from noninfected persons.

## SUPPLIES
### Food and Water
Due to the lack of a reliable means for testing food and water for contamination, it is best when unsure to switch to previously stored food and water. Food in airtight packaging can be used after the container is decontaminated. Water purification systems are a good investment, and vary in cost depending usually on the amount of water to be treated in a period of time. Water can be boiled for half an hour, or water purification tablets, preferably in a high dosage, can be used.

### Protective Equipment and Measures
The best time to buy protective equipment is long before a CBW attack happens, or even before the threat of such a attack is widely publicized. This is because during an emergency, there may be a shortage or even complete unavailability of protective equipment. Prices will also shoot up dependent on demand. Standard military and civilian gas masks and respirators protect against most, although not all, chemical and biowarfare agents. The same is true of more expensive bioprotective suits.

In the event of chemical or biowarfare attack or other contamination, dust masks or surgical masks may be effective. The simple procedure of using cloth or a towel as a covering for the nose and mouth may even be helpful. All exposed body areas should also be covered, including the hands. Raincoats and slickers may be of some use as protection, and even improvised protective clothing made out of plastic sheeting or even garbage bags is better than nothing.

Cuts, abrasions, and other wounds that penetrate the skin are areas that provide an entry point to the body for biowarfare agents. During the event of CBW warfare, care should be taken to protect against wounds to the body.

Any CBW shelter should be equipped with firearms for self defense.

## DECONTAMINATION

In many cases, it is safer to evacuate areas contaminated by CBW attack, and after you are in a safe area, to discard contaminated protection equipment. If this is not possible, there are three main methods of decontamination, defined as (1) mechanical, (2) chemical, and (3), physical.

### Mechanical

Washing and flushing with non-disinfectant liquid, such as water, since it does not kill bacterial contaminants, is termed a mechanical method. A simple shower or sponge bath using lots of hot water and soap can be effective in removing biological or chemical agents.

### Chemical

Chemical methods are considered to be more effective in decontamination than mechanical means. Living areas may be decontaminated with commercial brand disinfectants, such as the types used in hospitals. After decontamination, living areas should be ventilated before spending time in them.

Some of the types of commercial disinfectants that are available are isopropyl alcohol, diluted ammonia or chlorine solutions, chlorohexidine, formaldehydes, and glutaraldehydes. Inhalation of some of these chemicals can be harmful and so care should be taken in their usage. U.S. Army portable decontamination apparatus ABC-M11 (NSN 4230-00-720-1618) can be obtained inexpensively from some army surplus dealers. U.S. Army DS2 solution (Decontaminating Solution No. 2) is used with this equipment, and may also be obtained as surplus. DS2 is said to be effective against all known toxics and biological materials except spores, including VX.

If special disinfectants are not available, clothing should be washed with plenty of commercial detergent and bleach. Afterwards, clothing should be dried using the hottest setting on a clothes drier.

Alcohol is effective at killing living microorganisms, but will not kill spores. A commercial disinfectant like Lysol will also kill microorganisms, but may be ineffective against some spores, like anthrax.

For the decontamination of areas of landscape, one expert recommends a mixture of chloride of lye or lime.

**Physical**

Physical means for killing bacterial contamination include the use of heat, radiation, or sunlight. The best policy is to burn clothing that is contaminated. If this is not possible, boiling water or the use of a hospital autoclave may be useful for decontamination in certain instances. If boiling water is used, it should be kept at a boil for about one half hour. If an autoclave is used, it should be maintained at a 250 degree temperature for at least fifteen minutes. A hair dryer on its hottest setting may be useful in decontaminating skin, clothing, or other items. A household oven can be used to decontaminate nonflammable items. Another possibility for decontaminating smaller items is the use of a microwave oven. Clothing may also be hung outside to expose it to sunlight. Sunlight will kill most, although not all, biological agents.

A combination of methods of disinfecting may be desirable. For instance, contaminated or possibly contaminated fabrics may be boiled, and be physically scrubbed with a disinfectant such as household bleach.

There are a number of kits specifically designed for decontamination on the market today. These may be obtained from larger surplus stores or survival equipment suppliers.

## NOTES ON MEDICAL ASPECTS

Prior to a CBW attack, immunization against specific biological threats should be considered. This is a somewhat controversial area, in that vaccinations, particularly 'cocktail'-vaccinations in which a number of vaccines are injected together or in close succession, may in fact induce serious side-effects, as may have been a contributing cause to what is known as Gulf War Syndrome.

One should study current information on vaccinations, including 'heretical' views that will not be found in mainstream publications. Since the author of this book is not a doctor, I would not presume to make suggestions based upon my own beliefs in this matter. The individual should make his own choice based upon a thorough investigation of options.

It is also a good idea for individuals to have a cache of antibiotics on hand, and expertise in using them, in the event of CBW attack or even a naturally occurring epidemic. Supplies of this sort will rapidly become exhausted.

Professional medical care should be sought as soon as possible by persons after a CBW attack, although it also must be taken into consideration that hospitals or other areas with large numbers of sick persons should be avoided.